T0354788

Just
Messing Around

A Latchkey Kid's Tales of Growing
Up on Long Island in the 60s

ROBERT HODUM

JUST MESSING AROUND
A LATCHKEY KID'S TALES OF GROWING UP ON LONG ISLAND IN THE 60S

iUniverse books may be ordered through booksellers or by contacting:

iUniverse
1663 Liberty Drive
Bloomington, IN 47403
www.iuniverse.com
844-349-9409

Because of the dynamic nature of the Internet, any web addresses or links contained in this book may have changed since publication and may no longer be valid. The views expressed in this work are solely those of the author and do not necessarily reflect the views of the publisher, and the publisher hereby disclaims any responsibility for them.

Any people depicted in stock imagery provided by Getty Images are models, and such images are being used for illustrative purposes only.
Certain stock imagery © Getty Images.

All illustrations by Robert Hodum

ISBN: 978-1-6632-5600-3 (sc)
ISBN: 978-1-6632-6540-1 (hc)
ISBN: 978-1-6632-5601-0 (e)

Library of Congress Control Number: 2023917234

Print information available on the last page.

iUniverse rev. date: 09/06/2024

For Mom and Dad, my sister and brother and the rest of our brood, for our children and grandkids, and for this latchkey kid who remembers it all and wishes that we had had more time together.

Contents

A special thanks to my Happy for being an appreciative custodian of these stories and for lending her keen, editorial eye and clear understanding of the written word to their final preparation.

Your Bob

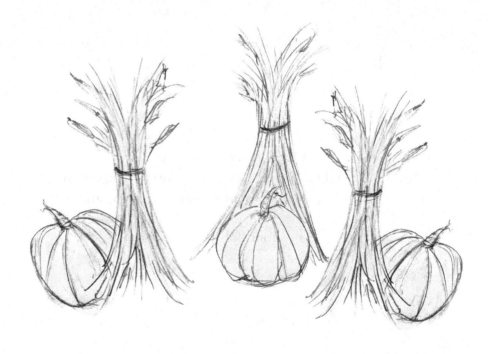

Just Like Water

oday I gave *time* a chance to be itself; fluid, unhinged, without sequence, like the blue autumn skies over this farmer's field. It appeared on the other side of my lunch break at a job I had taken at a Halloween attraction on Long Island's East End. The owner needed help with the preseason renovation of his haunted house, an old potato barn surrounded by farmland. I signed on to work until the end of September, the first fall of my retirement from teaching.

After eating, I stretched out in the shade along the treeline that bordered this farm. I ran my hands over the blades of grass on the rise that overlooked this expanse of sod and clouds. Sensing that I wasn't alone, I looked up. The field wavered in the heat of the noon sun. A shadow pushed forward, through memory echoes, imagination, and a sense of time that flowed just like water.

And there he was ... I was.

My childhood self waved at me from the middle of an East Northport potato farm. As a kid, I had stood in fields like this one, rubbing my feet deep into its soil. In my mind's eye, I sauntered along, stick in hand, my feet caked in mud, under cloudless, summer skies. Those skies stewarded my daily adventures. They drew us latchkey kids far up past the circling seagulls. We drifted on those clouds, looking down on the universe where we ran wild.

Suburbia hummed with novelty in the early sixties. The sounds at worksites in the nearby developments spoke of new families that would be coming to our little town of East Northport. Neighborhoods smelled of recently laid asphalt and the roads shone with freshly painted, broken white lines. So many newly poured foundations to climb down, framed-out houses left unattended to investigate, and recently dug sumps whose easily-scaled chain link fences led to sinistrous drainage tunnels! A well-set table of escapades and antics awaited us daredevils. We anticipated adventures as our daily course of events and learned to extricate ourselves from most of the trouble we provoked.

Those fields and wooded tracts bordered the outer limits of our known domain. Little did we care to know the other world beyond those treetops. Though it filled our socks and caked under our fingernails, we had no idea that the ground under those fields was timeless and our memories, unlike the dirt on our jeans, not easily washed away.

That world, turned under by decades of tractor wheels and largely covered by two-story colonials, still seeps up from this farmer's field today. The darkness of the surrounding woods whispers adventure, but also caution. Recollections of the conflict, isolation, anger, and fear that colored our childhood palettes lurk in the shadows of those trees like rusted, sharp-cornered tractors.

We latchkey kids were alone, marooned on islands of our own creation, where exhilaration frequently ended in laughter or fisticuffs. But for certain, those days concluded with an inevitable return to dark and empty homes. Sometimes we weathered well the loneliness and sense of abandonment that we came to consider normal. Other times, we did not.

We went to school with our house keys, dangling around our necks or tied to our belts, tucked away in change purses or stuck deep in pants pockets. Having lost mine twice in the first grade, my family hid my key under the milk box on our stoop. Responsible for locking up in the morning, turning lights out and radios off, and letting ourselves in after school, we kids did our best to convince ourselves that we were the keepers of the family's realm.

Locking up and leaving the house was easy for me. Anticipating the shenanigans of lunch and recess with buddies and the smiles of a few good teachers, I'd happily step away from my house. Though often scolded for being a dedicated clock-watcher, I'd crash out of school on the dot. That thrill of release and freedom didn't last long. My quick pace off school grounds slowed as I got closer to home. My arrival always ended the same, at a locked door. I dreaded entering that dark and empty house. Most of us latchkey kids shared that apprehension, rarely voiced to our parents, who expected us to maneuver deftly through that discomforting solitude.

Instead, we came up with strategies to survive that loneliness and conspired together to hatch adventures, raising a lot of noisy, unrepentant hell. We ran wild under those limitless, suburban skies. Whether I was solo or hanging with the gang, regardless of the weather or season, our antics played out in the neighboring fields and woods. This parentless world was our childhood's stage.

Today, I'm in time's debt for returning me to when my greatest concerns in life were dodging phone calls from my teachers, surviving roughhousing with my buddies, and barely getting home before my parents did. Always plotting new capers, skirting trouble, playing on the local hill, and digging tunnels deep into its soil, time seemed immutable, an eternal rollercoaster-run through seasons, adventures, and farm fields just like this one.

So, thank you, time, for allowing me to see life through the eyes of a child once again and find a return home.

Summertime Waifs

Absent parents and teachers, we were unshackled during the summers. Our parents left home early in the morning. The fathers of our neighborhood left by 6:30 to catch the morning train to Manhattan and returned home after 7 pm. Many of the moms, after dropping their husbands off at the Northport train station, were off to work before 7:30. That's what Mom and Dad did five days a week.

Dad started working for Socony Mobil Oil Company as a "runner" when he was eighteen-years old. A track star at Franklin K. Lane High School in Brooklyn, he qualified easily for this job which required him to run documents between the company's main office and the numerous depots and satellite offices throughout Midtown Manhattan. That was the beginning of his forty-year career with Mobil Oil. Years later after his promotion to General Office Manager, I'd see him seated at his desk at home, flipping through pages of hand-written columns of numbers. Dad did all his calculations in his head and his work in pencil.

Mom and Dad met in the building where they worked. She was a divorced telephone operator with an eight-year-old daughter. Dad was a widower with a son. After I was born, Mom stayed home to take care of me in our Glen Cove home. When I turned four, we moved out to East Northport. After my seventh birthday, she went back to work as a telephone operator for different businesses in Western Suffolk County.

During summer vacations, we kids, waifs from the early morning until dusk, were left to our own devices, entertainments, and deliciously nasty pursuits. Older siblings worked day jobs, so we kids followed *our* rules of conduct, forgetting Saturday Catechism lessons and parents' advisements, at least until the adults returned home. We gathered at 8 o'clock sharp weekday mornings under the branches of a weeping willow where we felt protected from unwelcome eyes. We'd make our plans, deciding what adventures to pursue and the level of risk we'd feel comfortable taking, and off we'd go. We wildings relished our summer days, playing outdoors, even in inclement weather.

Summertime fields smelled of wild wheat stalks that whispered in the breeze. Glistening vines of crimson poison ivy slithered up the corners of local farmers' sheds and wrapped around rusting farm equipment where we played hide-and-go seek. Blue skies, sweat-stained T-shirts, and the odor of earthworms after an early morning rain added to the colors and scents of our summers.

Our hideout, an abandoned trailer behind a neighbor's farm, was our final destination at the day's end. Its darkened interior conjured up images of ghostly October shadows, winter igloos of the far-off Arctic tundra, and pillboxes on some Japanese-occupied Pacific island. Its walls sucked in our stories of our sandlot baseball games, flipping baseball cards on the sly, who had the fastest bike in the neighborhood, and where we hid our very graphic *Mars Attacks* trading card collections that our parents had banned from our homes. An accounting of our most recent illicit activities usually figured at the end of these discussions; errant stones that broke neighbors' windows, recent playground fights, inventive curses, and who had gotten caught playing with fire.

And yes, we played with fire a lot.

Striking Matches

We kids mastered the art of playing with fire at an early age. Our parents considered the ability to light a match a valuable life skill, given that their childhood chores included lighting the gas sconces and wood stoves in their kitchens or parlors. As kids they dried their hair over metal heating grates in the floor and didn't have indoor plumbing. We children of privilege had to manage stirring soup on electric ranges, closing the doors of refrigerators, and remembering to turn off light switches. Unfortunately, the good and useful skill of striking a match led parents and children astray. *They* started smoking in their young adult lives and *we* played with fire.

Many of our parents were smokers. Dad lit up his first cigar at age twelve in the family's outhouse in Brooklyn. During his adulthood, Dad's birthdays or Christmas gifts included well-crafted wooden boxes of artistically-banded cigars. He'd end the day in his recliner with a cigar in his mouth and his grandfather's smoking stand close at hand. Mom and my sister always had some kind of menthol cigarette, and my brother rolled his pack of cigs in the sleeve of his white T-shirt when he went out with his friends.

I never liked their smoking habit. My clothes stank of cigar smoke so much that my childhood dentist once suspiciously inquired about my personal smoking habits. Once, after being admonished by my sister never to smoke, I pinpricked a pack of her cigarettes. Her first drag on one of those decommissioned cigarettes was worth the scolding.

My family's Sunday dinner conversations, ashtrays on the dinner table, sometimes strayed into muffled talk of Russian nuclear attacks and how we'd have to buy guns and stockpile food, water, and, of course, matches. It sounded like we kids might have to pull ourselves out of some crazy, war-imposed stone age, and being able to make fire would be integral to our survival. Though admonished never to take that skill lightly, matches opened new avenues of entertainment for me and my friends.

I acquired the match-striking skill quickly and soon became know as the go-to kid for little twig fires, igniting balsa wood planes before takeoff, and a general singeing of plastic model toys and army men when buddies needed things to look "authentic" for their set-ups. We recreated flaming dogfights with rubber band-powered balsa wood planes. Pouring a rivulet of gasoline on the tips of the wings, lighting it up, and hand launching the plane created a most impressive scene for our imaginary air  battles. Planes with their tail fins soaked in gasoline left fabulous smoke trails. One of us would strike the match and another would release the plane with a quick throw. We'd evaluate the burns and the crashes of these expendables, never realizing the horror that this must have meant in real life.

We did our best to recreate whatever we saw on Vic Morrow's TV show, *Combat!* or in any war movie that we might have seen in our local cinema. It either involved firecrackers, hard to acquire except in July, or gasoline, easily found next to the lawnmower in every kid's garage. Reality was we just liked burning stuff.

One day, I changed it up and decided to use tar roof shingles that Dad had lying around and build a miniature house that gave refuge to a squad of plastic soldiers. Simple enough but I decided to do this in our garage. Of course, I left the garage door open for ventilation. I wasn't sure whether tar would burn, so I poured some gasoline on for a dramatic flare. I struck a match and BOOM! The flames of a short-lived mushroom cloud reached taller than I stood. Once the fire died down to less than a foot high, I grabbed my dad's coal shovel and swatted the flames that set the metal shovel head on fire. So, I extinguished the fire by pouring the remnants of an open bag of cement on the flames. Midday during the summer, most parents worked, so the smoke that billowed out of the garage door never triggered a call to the fire department. The kids knew that I was just messing around.

I shoveled through the melted tar that had turned to a pottage of hot, black glue on the garage floor. The edge of the face of the shovel curled back and melted away as I scraped up the molten tar. I dug a hole in Mom's garden and buried the hardening tar sludge behind the last row of her roses.

By 5 o'clock in the afternoon, a dark smudge remained on the floor near our car's oil stain. A faint smell of smoke and tar lingered as I wiped the shovel off and stuck it behind the other tools. Remarkably, my folks never realized the pyrotechnics that had taken place that day in the family garage.

Tim, an older kid who lived the street over, hosted the greatest pyrotechnic event ever held on our block. A week before, we had all gone to the movies to see *Barabbas*, a film about a criminal who was pardoned by Pontius Pilate and later became a famous gladiator. We reenacted its battle scenes with swords crafted from the struts of winter fences that rotted along the perimeter of the farmer's field.

One of the film's Colosseum fight scenes featured a river of fire that the gladiators jumped over to reach their opponents. The weekend after the movie, Tim's father had trenched around their patio and had run metal conduit for electric lines for lamp posts to illuminate the area. Tim, ever the showman, called us over for a daredevil show when our parents were at work.

When we got there, he poured gasoline in the trench from end to end, told us to step back, and threw a match into the pit. A wall of flames took seconds to ignite and was just high enough for him to jump back and forth just like those gladiators. Tim invited us to try. With swords in hand, we spent the next couple of minutes jumping over the flames. With each leap, the fire got lower and lower, so he just kept adding gasoline, and we continued jumping.

Since Tim had gone through puberty before us, he could boast of having singed his leg hair. We just seared our already beaten-up sneakers. None of us noticed that the fire had charred the conduit and melted the exposed electric cable. He got some serious whacking when his father connected the damaged conduit and cable with the empty gas can. Tim didn't play with us for quite a while after that day.

Roaming the Fields

I grew up playing on potato fields. Sloshing in the mud, sometimes way over the tops of my sneakers, I chased butterflies, threw stones and sticks at anything that moved, and jousted with seagulls that dared to land in the large day-puddles that formed after a good rain. I felt like I floated above those fields, happily encased in that summer snow-globe world of piercingly clear blue skies.

Morning showers would leave pools of water in furrows that reflected a muddied kaleidoscope of sky. My eyes fixed on the clouds, and never pulling back my steps, I'd march over the furrows, disregarding the inevitable stumble to my knees. My outstretched hands usually kept my face out of the muck.

Some mornings from my backyard, I'd hear my buddies clubbing splashes out of the mud puddles in the low points of the field. I'd join in the splatter fest and embrace the mud and muck that came my way. Other times, with pointy sticks in hand, we'd harpoon the opaque water, hoping to spear whatever creature might be at the bottom of that miry sea. When I returned home, Mom would always order me to strip at the back door. I'd clap the mud off my sneakers and clothes and mound them off to the side. Despite her threats of spankings, mucky puddles never lost their appeal.

On sunny days, we'd hunt the much prized and ever dangerous bumble bee. Hunting bees became my specialty. We filled jars with the engorged, black and white ones that foolishly lingered over the swatches of clover that covered the field's borders. Scooping them up with those glass spaghetti sauce jars that we carried with us, we'd feed them tufts of clover or grass clippings. Some would even make it home alive. After their day's captivity, I'd dump mine out on the lawn before dinner, watching the hearty ones buzz away.

Sometimes we'd catch them in our cupped hands and quickly slap our palms on the tops of the open jars, hoping that the impact would dislodge the bee from the fleshy part of our hands. That usually worked. Having been stung several times, after the initial shock, I'd put on a brave face, say a few curses, and continue hunting. Out in those fields, surrounded by our friends, we'd try to pull out the stingers, assorted splinters, and thorns with our teeth and spit them away. We acted like the he-men we pretended we were; never a tear or a whimper.

But when our moms came at us with the tweezer's cold, silver claws of death, we'd scream our lungs out. You see, we were also very accomplished actors, and could turn on the tears and sobs whenever it suited us. Sometimes we'd practice this. Who knew whether we'd tug at their heartstrings and wrangle an extra serving of ice cream or tapioca pudding out of them. This never worked with our teachers, but at home, now that was different. One thing I learned, always choose your mom over an older sibling for the extraction.

All of the crap, the no-way-am-I-doing-that attitude, the snippy, wise-ass remarks, pushes, pinches, and general snootiness we'd give our siblings all came home to roost when an older brother or sister had the tweezers in their hands. The promises of never doing it again flowed as quickly as our real tears. And somehow they always walked away avenged and satisfied, and we, for the moment, repentant.

Bees weren't for all of us. A few of the kids collected the monarch or swallowtail butterflies that on good days, painted the ground in a levitating mass of color. They mounted those things on blocks of cardboard and had wooden cases full of these trophies. They even studied their names and points of origin. For most of us, they were just field butterflies, simple as that, and if we could pick them off with an accurately aimed stone or swat them with a tree branch, we did.

As long as the supply lasted, potato wars were high on everyone's list. We picked the discarded tubers out of the dried furrows. Some had already begun to rot and were perfect for potato-throwing "chuck battles". Others were edible. I remembered my mom telling us once how she and her friends would roast "mickies", potatoes thrown into small, open fires that they'd eat during the Depression. We opted to throw them, the more rotten the better.

Marksmanship was always a function of how you gripped the irregular mass of rotting potato. If the projectile were still fresh and hard, we'd pull our throws. After all, these *were* our friends that we pelted. But if that tater was soft and oozy, we let it fly as fast and as hard as the arm could throw. Overhand was a sure hit, sidewinder not so reliable. A direct hit was marked by a clamorous response from any witnesses, and a scream and a string of curses from the victim. Retribution was almost immediate from the wounded soul or one of his closet friends. So, you really never knew from what angle the potato was going to come.

Duck, turn, and run proved to be the best tactics during these potato wars. But never under *any* condition, did we ever aim at the face. If an errant throw happened to strike a buddy's face, an immediate and most sincere apology was offered. Gritting our teeth and pushing down any sense of triumph or laugh, we'd pat the shoulder of the victim. In extreme cases when his tears flowed and the slighted one was inconsolable, it was potato war etiquette to hold your arms out, offering up your body for a free shot. Of course, it was to be thrown from a reasonable distance, determined by the shouts of approval from the others to the one-man firing squad.

If you offered to take one in the chest to make peace, you couldn't move, flinch or duck. Doing so caused you to lose face, and you and your family paid for it for the rest of the day, being cursed in the most vile and inventive ways. But taking the potato blow meant that you were the unspoken king for the day. Though the title was short-lived, it earned you some deference, pats on the back, and a solid and warm *adieu* from the gang at the end of the day.

Ultimately, the tears of the swollen-faced victim dried quickly once vengeance had been exacted. The older kids insisted that handshakes seal the truce, allowing us to return the next day without grudges. Playing in those proving grounds separated gang leaders from their followers and reminded us that a handshake counted, at least until the next poorly aimed potato.

The Hill

During the construction of our new elementary school, the contractors mounded all the excavated soil in the old farmer's field directly behind my house. From the canopy of the wild cherry trees that ran the length of our property line, I watched the trucks piling foot after foot of dirt, spreading it out to the width of the infield of a baseball diamond until they completed the excavation for the school's foundation. By the end of the spring, we had our own Mt. McKinley. Never mind that we would eventually have swings, jungle gyms, and basketball courts on the school grounds. It was the hill that became our source of shared adventures and personal dramas, and our much valued and defended turf.

In the northern corner of a former potato field, now school property, and at a great distance from the recently completed Fifth Avenue Elementary School, the hill promised solace and adventure, a site for rendezvous, cloud watching, sleigh riding, and unrestrained tunnel digging. This was our domain, undeniably free of adult strictures, a netherworld of mystery constantly undergoing seasonal transformation. Pockmarked by the holes and tunnels that we dug, and sled trails that cut deep into its steeper sides, it was a place of wonder and refuge.

You'd swear that we were all sons and daughters of miners, given our skill for tunneling into its topsoil. We intuited its texture and pliability before shoveling out trenches and caves. We jumped, rolled, and crawled in its rich, dark soil. After a hard day's play, we carried dirt home in the cuffs and pockets of our pants, shirtsleeves, and sneakers. We wore its smudges and grains behind our ears and under our fingernails for days.

If we could have eaten the dirt, we would have. Certainly most of us inadvertently swallowed several handfuls over the years of rolling down its weed-covered embankments, throwing globs of mud, and cutting deep into its sides with our fathers' shovels. We dug trenches, caves, and tunnels as the weather became warmer and the spring rains loosened up the winter's compacted soil from our sleigh runs. Pockmarked like the battlefields of the Somme, the hill was our canvas, pliable to our spades and subject to our creativity.

From its summit, we could see people in their backyards, and whether friend or foe might be approaching. Its sloping sides provided a slip-slide run of cushioning weeds. We made beds from clumps of knee-high grass that rolled from the top, overlooking the nearby farmhouse. Grasshoppers abounded, bumblebees circled the stalks of flowered weeds that surrounded us, and long-legged spiders crawled over our chests.

We stretched out to watch the clouds in a summer sky. Those billowing, bedsheet clouds took shape and morphed into expendable delights, and then suddenly misted into oblivion. We painted on that canvas every imaginable shape and scene, each of us a Picasso in the making.

We'd hear our moms call us to dinner. One or two families had supper bells that inevitably clanged around 5:30. One father, an immigrant from Switzerland, would climb up on his roof and yodel to call his kids home. The parents couldn't see us, but instinctively knew the direction to shout their calls. Sometimes I caught glimpses of Mom stepping out onto the cement stoop directly off our home's kitchen. Her first call to eat would be inquisitive. The second was more strident, the third signaled annoyance, and would be certainly less forgiving than the first two. I didn't wait for the fourth.

All of us tried to delay our returns home. Grudgingly, we'd drop our rocks and sticks, and drag our shovels home in July's heat, pull our sleds over the frozen, weedy clumps in January, and grab our plastic or home-made weapons, dropping the caked mud bombs of October. We exchanged the obligatory *See ya* and headed off to home.

When my folks consigned me to my room for some transgression or rudeness, I'd look out my window and study the changing contours of the hill, and relive my most outstanding adventures there. Seen from my bedroom window on rainy afternoons and during winter snowstorms, the hill morphed, sometimes vanishing into the fog of rain or swirling snow. But the hill was eternal, and upon the storm's passing, it would reappear and wait anxiously for my next visit.

The Widow of the Woods

I spent many of my summer days walking farmers' fields and the nearby woods with the kids from our block. We'd kick fallen branches that we couldn't snap with our feet, skip stones on the brown puddles left by morning rains, probe animal carcasses with sticks, and, of course, tell stories.

We walked for hours, debating the merits of TV shows from the evening before, the strengths and weaknesses of our favorite comic book characters, and who amongst us fell dead the best when we played war. We filled our personal airways with this chatter, knowing it to be simply a prelude to the real discussion; where we'd go exploring and what adventures we'd have that day.

Funny that we never spoke of what went on in our homes. The problems our families faced and the issues we might have had with siblings went unmentioned. We rarely spoke of our onerous household rules and chores, and certainly never talked of how we were disciplined when we failed to comply. The sadness, troubles, and challenges that at times seemed to define our families went unmentioned and remained behind our homes' doors. Those silent realities we'd shed as we ran down the furrows of potato fields and sheltered in the coolness of the the oak trees that framed the entrance into our summer world.

Ever observant to the changes in the paths and fields of our surroundings, the banter let up when we scanned the horizon for the farmers and "the big kids" that more than once had chased us back home. Sometimes we'd walk without saying a word. We latchkey kids knew solitude all too well. Its weight of emptiness accompanied our morning breakfasts and waited for us as we returned from school in the afternoon. It paced behind our homes' doors, alert to the rise of a garage door or the turn of an unlocked doorknob.

For some of us kids, panic accompanied the first steps into an empty house. For others, the embrace of familiarity faded as the sense of being alone grew. A quick change of clothes and we'd be outdoors during temperate seasons, joined by every other kid whose parents and older siblings were not home.

As autumn darkened into winter, most of us resolved to hunker down, backs to the wall, and wait. Disquiet emanated from our attics and dispersed itself through the top floors. Its remains nestled in the darkened basement. Only the sound of a car in our driveways or the shuffle of our parents' footsteps behind an opening door relieved the isolation and separateness, and in some cases, the terror we felt during the winter months.

Though here in our woods, we sometimes chose to be quiet, if just for a while. Not imposed on us by others, this silence gave us a sense of fraternity and power. We controlled it as we explored these woods and footpaths that formed the nexus of our summertime world. A world where we never walked alone and quiet was not an enemy.

Surrounded by trees, some whose twisted trunks bore the scars of lightning strikes, we'd walk under their shade, along paths rutted deep by farmers' tractors. In daylight, their brown gnarled trunks and branches seemed to embrace us kids as we climbed up into their canopies. We'd occasionally discover in their bark, rusted and bent nails that must have held *No Trespassing* signs.

Those woods so familiar during the day turned sinister at dusk. They seemed to close ranks, forming a wall of mystery at night. They loomed menacingly along the roadway, even from the safety of the backseat of Dad's Chevy Impala as we returned Sunday evenings from my cousin's home in Kings Park. Never knowing what lurked in those shadows, we kids ruled out any visits after sundown.

A broken down house where an old lady lived stood at the entrance to the first grouping of trees across the street from our neighborhood. Known to us as *the witchy house*, an early 1920s two-story farmhouse with outbuildings had formed part of a once productive potato farm. It prowled in the shadows of the oaks that overhung her property. The owner, a woman widowed by a farming accident decades ago, appeared daily on her porch. She sat in a rocking chair, dressed in black with a gray apron tied loosely around her neck and waist. She spent her days staring up past the trees. Sometimes she'd glare at us as we sat on our bikes on the dirt path that bordered her once cultivated fields. Other times, unexpectedly, she'd thrash her arms to shoo us away. We'd stare back in silence, nod our heads, and move on. The locals who farmed these fields knew her as the Widow of the Woods. For us kids, she was a dark cloud that could pull us into the shadows if we failed to keep our teasing in check and frequent property invasions at a safe distance from her house. But sometimes we pushed it.

In the heat of those summers, the musty coolness of her collapsing barn was a major attraction for us. Distant from her front porch, we knew that she couldn't possibly get out there to grab us with those long, sharp nails that we imagined she must have had.

We'd climb up the hayloft's ladders to investigate the piles of rusting farm tools and stacks of old magazines and yellowing newspapers. Each of us took a turn swinging from a thick, coarse-threaded rope draped over one of the beams. Thinking that she was unaware of our shenanigans, we'd  run in and out of her barn, playing tag across her wilted gardens. More than once, we'd catch her glaring at us, studying our faces. One time, she rose from her rocker, leaned over the porch's railing, and pointed her finger unwaveringly … at me.

When school started our invasions of her property and our walks through the woods lessened and eventually came to an end. By the middle of September, Halloween seemed imminent. Its unvoiced presence accompanied the beginning of every school year at Fifth Avenue Elementary School. Halloween impatiently waited for us behind any events that the new school year might bring. Rushing through homework, memorizing lines for fall plays, fights on the playground, anticipating phone calls from teachers, and picking the right moment to ask my parents to sign the first quarter's report card were merely ambient noise.

Autumn was synonymous with Halloween. As pumpkins began to appear in local farmers' fields, the days grew cooler and leaves covered the ground. A palpable sense of abandon, mystery, and the unexpected could be found in the darkness of fall evenings. For us kids, that one night seemed to always be around us. Every unidentified creak, sinister shadow, and rustle in the leaves would magnify our already heightened sense of anticipation. All Hallows' Eve blushed our October evenings with this wonderfully, unsettling air.

Before we were of age for flying solo on Halloween, which was widely agreed to be nine years old, a parent or an older sibling assumed the role of a chaperone. I considered advocating for an early release, but my folks had made it clear that until my teacher stopped calling them about my questionable behavior, I'd be walked around the neighborhood with a very firm hand. But let's be clear about this, no matter how much we kids might have protested having an escort, we were secretly relieved that we weren't allowed out alone. As I discovered, these chaperones didn't mean that hair-raising encounters wouldn't happen.

All seemed under control one Halloween when Fran, my sister, escorted me to the houses in our neighborhood. She held my hand as I did my rounds and coached me on how to knock firmly if there was no response to the ringing of the doorbell. She discretely waited at the curb as I marched up to the door and knocked, shouting *Trick or Treat*.

At first, there were plenty of kids out that night, most accompanied just like me, but as the evening progressed the sounds of other children faded away. As we made our way up Chandler Drive towards Pulaski Road, the main thoroughfare that boarded the woods, my sister seemed anxious to get home.

We were six house-lengths from the old lady's farmhouse that stood among the trees on the opposite side of the street. It had started to drizzle and the leaves were wet, glimmering in the moonlight. Homeowners began to turn off their porch lights and close their front doors, thinking that we kids had all gone home. It would have been pitch black if it weren't for the light of the full moon.

Now all I could think of was how that old witchy lady would be waiting in her rocking chair, glaring down from her porch at me, waiting, just waiting for the right moment to strike. As we approached her home, I imagined her rising slowly from her rocker, dressed all in black. She would turn towards me and glare unblinking as I walked past her porch. Suddenly with uncharacteristic speed, she would be standing behind a tree on my side of the street, her hands and witchy nails visible around the tree trunk closest to me, and then she would lunge!

The quieter it got on this street, the more real this scenario seemed. As the wet leaves muted our steps, the more distinct became the sound of her nails scratching the tree trunk nearest us. If I had spoken to Fran about any of this, the witch would surely have heard me and acted accordingly. So I kept quiet and walked a little quicker.

Just as we were about to turn the corner onto our street, Fran stopped and pulled me tightly to her side. I was looking across the street at the old lady's porch and could see some kind of movement over there.

"Did you see *that*?" Fran whispered, pointing up at the moon.

I looked at the tree trunks nearest us, searching for those gnarled fingers that surely ended in those long, knife-like fingernails, but I saw nothing.

"There it is *again*, Bobby!"

She was pointing up at the moon, her eyes seemed focused on the dark around the glow.

"I saw her. I saw something fly right across the face of the moon. It was a black shape moving fast across the moonlight! Keep looking, now. You'll see her!"

Believe me, I didn't want to see her, but I looked long and hard for anything that I could report to my sister. The wind had picked up and the clouds started to move in the moonlight, the leaves and the trees rustling.

And that's when I heard a creaking sound, incredibly distinct, seeming to move with the wind. It sounded like the rocker on the porch of the "Widow of the Woods."

"Did you hear that, Fran?"

"No, Bobby, I didn't hear a thing, not at all."

I scanned the trees at the corner; saw no movement, no hands, and no fingernails. I started to pull my sister to move faster, and then I looked up at the moon.

At first it appeared to hover just out of the ring of moonlight, but slowly, very clearly, a black shape tracked across the face of the moon, and disappeared out of the light and into the darkness of the night sky. I was afraid to look back.

I started running down the street, hoping that I'd make it to my stoop and front door before those fingernails could reach me.

My sister, in pursuit, called out, "Bobby, slow down. It's all right. Stop running!"

I was at my door and in the house, calling for my parents long before Fran made it to our front yard.

When she came in, I was seated at the kitchen table telling Mom and Dad about the creaking rocker, the fingernails, and the flying silhouette across the moon. They assured me that it was only trees scraping up against one another and only the night winds blowing clouds past the shining moon. I was unconvinced.

I wanted to tell Fran and my parents about how that old witchy lady of the woods would stare at us from her porch and once, even pointed her finger in my direction, how she seemed to know us, seemed to know me! But I knew those encounters had to remain unmentioned.

Several Halloweens later my parents announced that if I wanted to, I could go out on my own, barring school reports of bad behavior. All of us kids hoped to hear these words after our ninth birthday, and here it was, solo runs were finally sanctioned. The countdown scraped along the first weeks of October. By the third week, our many revisions of costumes, schemes of trickery, and jostling for leadership of the night's outing feverishly occupied our time. Finally, the day had arrived.

That morning Miss Ross, our music teacher, wisely chose Halloween songs for us to bellow. After she rolled her piano out of our classroom, our teacher recognized that we inmates had taken over. She pulled out the orange, yellow and black construction paper, scissors and glue, and sent us merrily on our way. Ordered to produce seasonal icons, we plastered the place with the most horrific scenes possible.

Finally the night had arrived. My parents reviewed all the rules, warnings and consequences, as I fidgeted with my costume. My sister looked at me and smiled. She walked me to the door. Fran seemed disappointed that she wouldn't be taking me out anymore.

I stood at the front door, costumed, with pillowcase in hand. I reminded her of that night and asked whether she really had seen anything. She gave me a look of certainty and surprise that I had even doubted the events of that night, and said, "Bobby, remember, keep your eyes on the moon and don't forget that anything is possible on Halloween."

"And by the way," she bent down and whispered, "I hope you kids left that widow alone this summer."

As I stepped out onto the stoop, she half smiled, winked, and closed the front door.

Messing Around

"See you at the hill" was the afternoon mantra that we'd shout at the end of another school day. We were learning the joys of being part of the gang and relished that sense of belonging to a tribe. But there was always a price to pay for that solidarity. The oldest would initiate the younger ones with some type of minor brutality for which they would ask forgiveness at the close of the day. They'd push past the initiated who was holding back tears and murmur to him as they headed home, "Sorry about that. Don't tell your mom."

Moms were the enforcers on our block. Most dads got home late and spent their weeks battling in the city. They rarely took local rifts to heart. True enough, but the moms wouldn't hesitate to ring a transgressor's doorbell and denounce misbehaviors or other assorted misdemeanors. Their timing was impeccable. They'd show up during dinner and you'd be trapped at the table. Getting up would have been an admission of guilt. Best thing to do was steel yourself, do your best to hear the conversation at the door, wait for the scream, and use your few words as adroitly as possible to delay the thrashing.

We all knew what we'd done, no mystery there, and pleading innocent was too transparently false. Denials and too many words only compounded the gravity of the punishment. Just sit there and take it. Crying was not an option, although I must say we all resorted to it on occasion.

Child rearing usually involved a healthy dose of corporal punishment. Everybody got hit for not only the infraction, but also for embarrassing the family. Slaps across the face were one technique, very public, noisy and quick, and were usually a response to foul language, disrespectful comments, and threatening a sibling. One slap usually did it, and was almost always well deserved. If they considered the infraction to be greater, and on that list there were a host of them, parents employed the belt or the wooden spoon. In my home, to add insult to injury, I had to remove my own belt or get the wooden spoon out of the kitchen drawer. The anticipation was generally worse than the pair of whacks I'd be apportioned. It unquestionably hurt my parents as much as it did me, and the punishment was later followed by an admonishment of sorts that reinforced the whacking, and almost always, a hug or a kiss. All of us kids got whacked. It was the way of the world.

I'd learn my lesson until the next time I'd put a rock through a school window, play with fire, steal someone's bike for a joy ride or give someone a glass of cold water drawn from the toilet bowl. Yes, that last one was a real "headshaker" and cost me two red butt cheeks, but it seemed like a great idea at the time. Most of the parents expected that sometime before puberty, whatever that was, the message to do right would be learned. We kids knew that they expected better behavior from us. It was just so hard towing the line.

We'd jump off roofs, cut off the heads of the neighbors' flowers, unscrew Christmas light bulbs from our neighbors' decorations and pop them on their doorsteps, and have crab apple wars with fruit that we harvested from ornamental shrubs. We'd throw rocks, bottles, pipes, 2x4s, shingles (our childhood Frisbees), which could be thrown a great distance, and would cut when they hit you. Once in the heat of the summer, with sharpened sticks as spears, we ran naked through the woods just to see what it was like to be cavemen. We chucked ice balls during the winter and "itchy balls" in the spring, and dirt bombs all summer long. So much for peace and tranquility in the suburbs!

Rocks, dirt bombs, those hardened pieces of mud that sailed so easily through the air, and switches or tree limbs fashioned into rifles were always in our hands. We relived every war story that our uncles or fathers had told us and reenacted scenes from the most recent war movie or science fiction film we had seen in the local movie house.

We'd climb on the picnic tables in our backyards and sail off to

25

tropical islands, fending off sharks, and Moby Dick-like white whales. We loosened the nails in the cross beams of those tabletops and benches, rocking them back and forth in tsunami-like waves. We snapped broom-handle paddles in half as we fought creatures spawned by typhoons. We battled Japanese frogmen, kicking them off our sinking PT boat, and fought off crews from Nazi U-boats. All of us took turns rolling off the deck into the churning waters, screaming to be saved. An outstretched arm always pulled us to safety, and though precarious as our situations might have appeared, we always fashioned a victory against impossible odds.

At the end of those sessions, we'd lay back on the well-worn picnic tabletops, chatting about recent episodes of the newest TV shows like *The Twilight Zone* or *Outer Limits*. We created new scenarios and villains for our favorites, watching every episode on our black and white TVs without fail, homework done or not. There were only four or five channels, but their shows were as much a part of our lives as were our families. *The Man from U.N.C.L.E.* could have been a distant relative. We all knew the characters' names and loved to imitate their voices. Alfred Hitchcock looked like a grandfather who we'd seen going into a neighbor's house for Sunday dinner.

War figured in much of our play. We fashioned every imaginable weapon from branches, strips of snow fencing, broken plastic toys or discarded tools. Making ray guns, spears, rifles, machine guns, cannons, grenades, and bows and arrows was second nature to us. If we had any red paint, we festooned swords with handles and sharpened tips with the blood of fallen gladiators, Confederate soldiers, Nazis or Japanese kamikaze shock troops. We saw our blood only when we over enthusiastically threw ourselves into bushes or didn't pull our punches or stabs with wooden bayonets.

Our understanding of war was purely anecdotal, gleaned from movies and TV. Our portrayals of heroes infrequently involved their deaths and foes always fell vanquished. Though we acted out being shot and dramatically collapsed on the ground with simulated death throes, all fatalities resurrected for the next scene, wounds were bloodless and healed instantly. Though we often played at war, we understood so little of the reality of any of it.

Most of our fathers, uncles or older brothers who might have experienced any of this firsthand, didn't discourage this play. Perhaps they saw it as a youngster's expression of patriotism. But there were a few who silently turned away. All we kids knew was that Americans never lost and we thought that heroes never died.

Our play scenarios never included atomic warfare. Blistering death rays from invading Martians and combating giant praying mantises or monster ants figured most certainly in playtime. But Russians and nuclear bombs were conspicuously absent from our playtime agenda. Though sometimes we discussed news events, which included our new nemesis, the Soviet Union. I remember we kids would talk about who in our group would survive going off to war. We wondered which neighbor might build a bomb shelter and how something invisible like radioactivity could be worse than a bullet. I never felt better after these talks, just worried. I knew there'd be no bomb shelter in my basement.

Anyway, this nuclear war threat was drummed into us in school, but not mentioned much at home. At the dinner table when I talked about our school's bomb drills and short films with scenes that showed homes and trees burning, bending, and exploding in the nuclear shockwave, Mom and Dad changed the topic. They'd ask whether I had been sent to the principal's office that day or whether I had any homework. My sister, Fran looked down at her plate, quiet. Harry, my older brother, was already stationed in Norfolk, Virginia, one of the East Coast's largest naval bases.

If I ever wanted silence at dinner, particularly if I suspected that my teacher might have called or had sent a note home about me, I knew what to bring up for a quick reprieve or at least a few moments of silence before the real shock wave hit.

None of us kids ever doubted that we'd somehow survive a nuclear attack. We'd still play baseball and ride bikes, no matter what. One of the big kids on the block bragged that his family installed a basement bomb shelter, complete with cinder block walls and a metal door. It was supposed to be a secret. So, he swore us to secrecy and shared his family's rules for survival: only family allowed when the sirens sounded, leave the dog outside, and, he made this very clear, if anyone tries to get in, don't open up, and any intruders that are successful, should be shot. When we asked whether he'd shoot us, he said firmly, "No one gets in except our family."

Maybe it wasn't the Russians that posed the worst threat. Neighbors would shoot neighbors and this older kid that I liked but feared now more than ever might have to shoot me. I was saddened that he would feel obligated to do that.

When his folks weren't home, he would invite us over and we'd rummage through their bomb shelter, imitating the shrill of a siren and closing the metal door with a bang. Last time we were down there, I saw a rifle leaning against a crate of canned food.

His comment made all this talk of nuclear war and radiation, the "duck and tuck" and sheltering drills in elementary school and our teachers' survival tips very real and frightening. At first our teachers instructed us to squeeze under our desks, face away from the windows, and remain silent. Later that drill was changed and we had to exit to the hallways, curl up, knees tucked tight with arms covering our heads, and lean against the wall. No one laughed or joked.

Once I asked my fourth grade teacher whether this drill would really protect us. Though she often had to discipline me, I liked and trusted her. She looked straight at me, and whispered, "Imagine the fires of Hell rushing down these halls. What do *you* think?"

Sledding on the Hill

S now came joyously heavy most winters, covering our old haunts and hiding places. Walking to school after overnight storms concerned our parents, but we saw this as an adventure in the making. I never understood why our parents bemoaned the evenings' forecasts of early morning snow. I'd get up early and listen for the siren that would sound around 7 o'clock. No announcements came across the radio or the TV. We home-alone kids lived on an informational wild frontier. Snow days were announced by the blasts of the fire house's siren but weren't always heard. Sometimes their silence went unheeded. More than once I didn't hear them, and walked to school, trudging through snowdrifts sometimes hip-high, only to find the doors locked.

Our winters were truly transformative and brought uninterrupted snow cover from the end of November to the beginning of March. During one unforgettable winter, heavy snows drifted to the roof of our one-story elementary school. We had no school for almost a week. Some kids tried to climb up the snow drifts onto the roof but they sank down to their chests, screaming to be pulled out.

Winter storms always transformed our hill into a sleigh rider's paradise. Heavy snows were emblematic of every December, January, February, and early March. We could count on at least four or five substantial snowfalls. The latter half of March was the big thaw and April, believe it or not, did have sunny, warm days and intermittent showers. The seasons were unfailing in their weather and timing, and we relished it all, most particularly those winter storms.

If one kid headed to the hill, we'd assume a snow day had been called. I'd wait to see the first kid open his garage door with sled in hand and head out to the hill. Like a Pavlovian whistle response, I'd rush to the garage, grab my galoshes, gloves, pull on my snowsuit, and trek out to the hill with my sled.

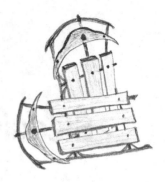

We had names for our sleds, the more ambitious and threatening the better. *Ramrod,* written in black paint on the front of the hard wood frame of my sled said it all. Its waxed metal runners glistened, assuring me of speed and danger for sure. We didn't just sled, we crashed our way down the slopes of the hill in wintry demolition derbies, taking out anyone to the side, rammed those in the front, and braced ourselves for attacks from behind.

If the snow had fallen heavily, I'd follow the tracks of the first kid out to the hill, crunching and stomping the path, deeper and wider for my return before sundown. There would be only a few of us early-morning sleigh riders. We diehards braved the frigid, morning winds and faint sun. But soon, the morning would warm up and the hill would be covered with kids and their speeding sleds.

We'd form sled trains, hitching our boots into the spaces of the metal frames near the steering ropes of the sled behind us. These rare moments of collaboration usually disintegrated before we'd reach the bottom of the hill. Plastic sleds and flying saucers weren't used in our neighborhoods yet, however some kids had toboggans and would blast past the individual sleds with ease. Time was not an issue for us. The morning turned into the afternoon, which muted into dusk. No lunch was eaten. Parents were at work and we were adrift. Schedules meant nothing to us at all. Only twilight signaled the arrival of our parents and the end of our day.

Moms generally came home first. Soon, just before sunset, the distinctive calls to dinner would echo out over the field. Few kids hesitated to take one extra run as the sun went down. With goodbyes said, and our parents' calls more harsh, we'd sled down and out across the well-compacted snow and head home. The great runs of the day were on my mind as I trekked along the morning's snowy path, reduced to a few inches of glistening, muddied snow in the early evening's cold.

I'd leave my sled out back next to the door. School or not, I'd be back out there, knowing that the night's freeze would make the ruts that cut into the hill much icier and faster the next afternoon. Stripping off my boots, gloves, and snowsuit, my mom would remark at how raw and red my thighs were and how lucky I was not to have frostbite. *Snow and the cold can kill ya*, she'd say.

Mom would remind me how Grandma Cross, when she was a kid had luckily survived the Blizzard of 1888, and that snow had reached the second floor windows of their home in Brooklyn. Many had run out of food and coal for their stoves, some had frozen to death. I thought that was always just a story, like so many others, until one time winter came hard to our lives.

Mom commuted thirty minutes to work every morning and no matter what the weather, she couldn't take time off. One afternoon she was later than usual coming home from work and I was worried. Turns out that Mom's car had spun out into a snowdrift and she had to walk three miles home, no boots and no gloves. When she got in, she was out of breath, soaked, and sat shivering at the kitchen table. I got her towels, made her tea. I rubbed her hands, and tried to calm her down. She was just so red in the face. Mom looked scared. She was worried about me and how I'd be alone. She worried about *me*!

I felt useless, and guilty. I had spent the late afternoon sleighing. Dad couldn't get home from the city that night and slept in his office. That storm was a bad one.

I still enjoyed sleighing at the hill with my buddies. But walking home the rest of that winter, I'd stare back at it. Notched deep by our sleds, it stood silent. How much it must have wanted us to return! I imagined that it felt alone and abandoned, as it disappeared slowly under the dark blue of those winter evenings.

A Snowy Night's Walk

For some reason there was an enormous disconnect between logic and Santa. All disbelief was suspended at the mere mention of his name. From the first door opened on our Advent calendar to the cookies and hot milk on Christmas Eve, Santa and all things magical were everyday considerations in school, out of school, before bed, and upon rising from it during the month of December. And, of course, being good weighed heavily on me.

I was frequently reminded that teasing my sister, not helping with the dishes, not taking out the garbage and forgetting to bring in the garbage cans was noted by Santa's helpers, the ever-present, yet invisible elves. Christmas vacation always gave us a day or two for reparations before the blessed morning. There was plenty of time to try and set things right, remember my chores, and be in as cheery a mood as I could muster. Baking cookies, making window paintings made with stencils and white, water-soluble furniture polish were the days' activities. The sound of wrapping paper crinkling behind closed doors was the final sign that Christmas Eve was approaching. Picking out the tree, one of my favorite activities, was a sacred privilege, which had to be accompanied by "perfect" behavior.

I particularly remember one tree-buying outing. It was a late

Saturday afternoon, and dusk had fallen quickly. Bundled up against the cold, my parents, sister Fran, Aunt Mae and I decided to take a walk to the Ketcham farm and its worn, rust-red barn to buy that year's Christmas tree. It had snowed in the morning and later that afternoon, and the roads were slippery. But it was unanimous that despite the wind and cold that night, such a beautiful winter evening had to be experienced firsthand. We set out on foot, slogging through the snow.

Few plows made runs after Saturday morning, so I felt like a frontiersman as I pulled my sled that would carry our tree home. Huddled in the tightest single-line formation we could manage, under a full moon, we headed east on Pulaski Road. The snow glistened, hanging heavy in the oak and maple trees along the route. Looking at our neighbor's old farmhouse, over their porch and into the draped front window, we could see the glow and flickering of a fire in their living room and the pastel lights of their Christmas tree.

We passed their property line and followed the path along the shoulder of the road. The stars were strikingly bright that night as we headed to the faint flicker of Christmas lights that outlined the roof of the red barn. The occasional car with snow chains on its tires would jangle past us in slow motion, challenged by the icy roads. Somehow we seemed to keep pace with the vehicles that inched their way past us. Some waved their approval of our Christmas walk. Others warded us off the road's shoulder and onto the snow banks with a polite but firm honk.

My mom spoke of Christmas angels that traveled with us that night. Dad's cigar smoke trailed out of the corner of his mouth, as he pulled the sled that had grown too heavy for me to pull. He told me to climb on. His smoke formed blue fragrant clouds in the freezing night's air. My sister had our dog, Tex, on a leash. He insisted on pulling her away from the path. Tex must have smelled the animals in the old barn. As he got closer, his short legs pushed harder through the snow. Aunt Mae hummed her favorite carols as I sat on my sled and looked up at the stars, feeling the evening snowflakes brush my eyelashes.

"It's going to snow heavy tonight," I whispered as we crossed the snow-covered street and entered the dirt entrance of Ketcham's barn.

Mr. Ketcham, one of the several farmers in our area who owned great fields of potatoes, sold Christmas trees and wreathes from his barn. His fir and pine trees were the most aromatic on those winter evenings, when our nostrils had become acutely sensitive to those aromas in the crisp winds. The barn's loft was filled with hay left over from autumn. The stalls that once housed cows and horses were storage for tools and small machinery that he and his sons used in the spring and summer. A steel drum outside the entrance had a fire blazing in it, warming the Ketcham boys as they waited for us to pick out our tree.

I don't remember who chose that year's tree. I know we always consulted Aunt Mae who traveled down from Hartford, Connecticut for Christmas. Her mild and gentle manner prevented her from making a definitive choice, and she deferred to her younger brother, Dad, who looked at Mom, who turned to Fran, who was trying to keep Tex, the mutt, from rooting in the stale hay at the barn's entrance. I'm sure that *I* gave an opinion. Finally the choice was made, and we loaded and tied the tree to my sled.

As we moved away from the barn and headed back home down Pulaski Road, snowflakes began to accumulate on the branches of our wonderful Christmas tree. Snow started to fall heavier and the wind whipped up. Our return trip home was punctuated with promises of hot chocolate and the occasional admonishment to those who complained about the cold and that happiness doesn't come without a cost. I was cold, kept my mouth shut, and struggled through the snow.

All I saw were the backs of my parents, Dad pulling the sled with the tree and my mom struggling with Tex as the growing snowdrifts swamped his Corgi frame. My sister pushed her boots through the accumulating inches of snow. Aunt Mae slogged forward, humming her carols. We trudged along the side of the road nearest the Miller family's house, and I used its lights as a mental place marker. I knew that relief was around the next corner as we passed the Miller's homestead and turned down our street. My chunky thighs, covered in my husky-sized pants, were stinging from the wet and cold. And tonight's pleasure would be exacted in cold feet, tired legs, and nearly frostbitten fingers. But we had our Christmas tree!

I felt so close to my family, walking through that snowstorm. My folks were right about insisting that we walk to get the tree. They had grown up, living by simple axioms; everything had a cost, hard work, sacrifice and discomfort usually preceded enjoyment, and simple pleasures were often treasured the most of all. And if you were lucky, all *that* was made more memorable by experiencing it with loved ones.

After the hot chocolate and toasted bread with honey and cinnamon had been finished, and my thighs glowed a little less red from the cold, I was tucked into bed and told to give in to sleep. But, I stayed awake, reliving that night's walk with my family. That would be my most cherished, childhood Christmas moment.

A Different Kind
of Christmas

I remember one Christmas that felt unlike the others. Dad and I decorated the two pine trees at the front door of our house with the large colorful bulbs that we stored in the crawlspace closet in the basement. Behind that magical closet's gray door all of the Christmas decorations patiently waited until the day after Thanksgiving. It was truly the inner sanctum of all that was Christmas, and its opening signaled the beginning of the season.

We'd stretch the strands of outdoor lights across the basement floor, testing each set and replacing the bulbs that had broken filaments. Replacement bulbs of vintage colors, shifted in a worn Macy's box, each clattering for its turn on the Christmas stage. The lighting of each length of Christmas lights painted the basement kaleidoscopic.

Standing on my toy chest, I could see boxes of ornaments tucked into the far corner of the crawlspace closet. Its darkness was scented by the smell of dried orange rinds and over-seasoned candy canes that wafted out from one of the boxes that held our Christmas stockings.

On Christmas morning, oranges plumped out the bottoms of our stockings, buried by balsa wood planes, kidney-red bouncy balls, and plastic paratroopers with colorful parachutes. I never ate that fruit, but found it fascinating that Santa had chosen them as one of his preferred treats. They'd wind up in the kitchen fruit bowl by Christmas afternoon. Most candy canes rarely made it past Christmas morning.

Their sweet aroma unmasked the few broken survivors from last year that lurked at the bottom of a random ornament box or stocking.

Several days before that Christmas Eve, Mom and I stopped at Gitzsa's year-round farmstand, its four walls decorated for the season. It was painted green with plastic sheathing covering the windows and fruit bays that sucked in and out with the movement of the evening wind. Christmas trees, wreaths, and produce lined the walls and bins.

In one of the corners, separate from the cash register, there was a selection of toys boxed in their original see-thru plastic covers, stacked on dusty produce shelves. They seemed out of place for this market. This certainly wasn't Charles and Sons' Five and Dime store downtown in Hewitt Square, and certainly not Macy's or A&S where all highly sought-after toys were sold.

My mom seemed to halfheartedly examine the fruit while watching me stare at the toys. I showed a particular interest in a Hasbro Nike missile launcher. She noticed the discounted hand-written price on the box.

Suddenly, she was standing alongside me and in a low voice whispered, "You know, Bobby, this year's been rough on Santa, and he won't be bringing many toys."

This seemed to have been weighing on her since we got in the car and drove to this farmstand that we rarely frequented. She didn't speak, her silence filled by the seasonal music on the radio during our drive. Mom loved the holidays, and always wanted to give us kids and our relatives "a good Christmas" as she'd often say. Whatever family drama happened during the year, and there was always something, all of it could be erased, and a clean slate started with this gift that she worked hard to give us all.

It was something that I believed too, despite all the trouble I caused or got sucked into, the fights and arguments, the teachers' phone calls home, and the scolding and well-deserved whacking that I'd gotten. My misbehaviors that my folks never knew about, but that I carried within me, would be wiped clean by Mom's promise of a good Christmas. This, I hoped most of all.

I remember saying, "It's okay, Mom. Whatever Santa brings, will be great."

Her response, "Oh, Bobby, that's wonderful!" seemed out of place.

"Well, why don't I help Santa by buying this? You don't mind, right?" she asked, lifting the box from its shelf.

I followed her to the register.

"No, Mom, its fine."

After all, Santa was always watching and knew whether I had or hadn't been *wonderful* throughout the year. He certainly had seen how much I liked this battery operated ICBM launch pad. I never wondered whether he'd find it curious that this season dedicated to the King of Peace was sometimes celebrated with toy replicas of weapons of war.

I remembered how that October we feared that my brother's Navy destroyer would be called up to blockade and intercept Russian ships. In school we prepared for nuclear war through the fall and into the winter, not that we understood what any of that would really mean. But we did see the anxiety and uncertainty in the eyes of our teachers as we knelt, heads to the wall in the school's hallways. Maybe the true gift of a good Christmas was being able to forget all that, and not even think about how lucky we were that none of that had happened.

Taking out imaginary Russian Migs with rubber-tipped missiles occupied much of that Christmas morning. After lunch we watched Laurel and Hardy in *Babes In Toyland*. Later that evening, I got lost in the glow of the colored bulbs and their reflection on the strands of tinsel that chromed our tree. I'd squeeze under the tree and stare up into the lights, wondering what it would be like to live up in those branches.

When I thought no one was looking, I'd sneak some strands of tinsel off the tree and stretch and pull them back and forth over my forehead, like a tug of war rope-pull during the spring Field Day at school. The faster I'd pull the ends, the darker the smudge line I'd have midway between eyebrows and hairline. I'd swagger around displaying my forehead, trying to avoid Mom who'd laugh, lick her thumb, and rub the smudge away. She looked happy, sitting on the arm of Dad's easy chair, hugging him.

This was a good Christmas. Thanks for this gift, Mom.

Watching Wrestling
with Grandma

Grandma Cross was a big woman, weighing in at over two hundred and twenty pounds. She had large, work-tough hands and the voice of a traffic cop. She always smelled of cooking lard and bleach. When she hugged me, I'd disappear into the folds of her arms as she'd say, "How ya doin' kid?" I can't recall her ever saying my name on the Sundays she came for dinner. Grandma plopped herself at the kitchen table and led the discussions as the women of the family prepared our Sunday meal.

Grandpa would light up a cigar and walk the backyard. Sometimes if there was a game on TV, he'd find Dad's easy chair and settle in for a conversation-free, cigar-heavy afternoon. Dad, after the pleasantries were given, would find a comfortable spot on the couch and read the paper. Sometimes I'd see him at his desk upstairs doing pages of pencil-written calculations for Monday morning meetings.

Grandma and I didn't exchange many words on those Sundays. She'd be mostly silent during dinner. I'd be seated next to her and endured the occasional elbow nudge, admonishing me to sit up and eat "like a human being." After, she'd sit back and watch imperiously as Dad did the dishes and I dried them. I'd get a wink from her as I finished my kitchen chores. Her silence and mask-like countenance puzzled me because I knew the other side of Grandma that most of my family didn't.

On our Saturday morning visits to my grandparents, I'd hear her yelling at the playroom TV as it blared out the introductions of the day's wrestling matches. Yes, my stoic Sunday Grandma Cross was a Saturday wrestling fanatic.

When she heard us come in she'd call, "Bobby, you come down here now. We're watching wrestling!" On Saturdays, *the kid* had a name.

I'd find her seated on her favorite wicker chair with an embroidered cushion, wearing her morning dress, only a few feet from the TV screen. She'd grab me and sit me on her lap and, with her hairy-lip kiss, we'd start our visit, screaming at the antics of the wrestlers whose bios she knew by heart, booing that day's villains, and rooting for her favorites. That was when Grandma Cross was her most animated and conversant, at least with me.

The whole family knew her as the tough Scotch German woman, daughter of a Brooklyn dairy farmer. She was as big and as strong as her brothers who had worked the family farm. No one in the family messed with her. Even cousin Dennis knew that she was the force in the Cross household and always had been. Grandpa might have had the gun, but she had the iron will. I just loved these sessions and snuggled right up to her and followed her lead. I really had no idea who the heck these guys in tights and short shorts were. Didn't matter, I got to scream at the black and white images with her.

One thing you didn't do during these matches was root for the opposition. And Grandma made it really clear who that was or wasn't. So, I quickly learned that Haystack Calhoun, the burly, bearded, bear of a man, always shirtless and barefoot and dressed in farmer's jeans, was her favorite.

Calhoun, weighing in at over four hundred pounds, would bash his opponents with his belly or absorb the opposition's blows with his barrel chest. His signature move was to throw them down on the canvass and sit on them. He usually won.

Pretty Boy George, a handsome blonde with a weightlifter's physique was Haystack's nemesis. The women loved him in his skimpy wrestling trunks. He'd blow kisses to them, as he'd sneak some kind of sandpaper out of his shorts and rub it in the eyes of his opponent. He'd win a lot of matches but never against Haystack.

The Chief, an American Indian who dressed in full-Indian attire, headdress and all, would use his hands to tomahawk chop the necks of his opponents. After vanquishing his foe, he'd do a war dance around the ring. But my personal favorite was The Jamaican Kid, a Black dwarf whose signature head-butt, known as the "Coco Butt", sent even the full-size wrestlers reeling. Sometimes he'd be literally thrown out of the ring into the stands, but he'd always bounce up, jump back into the ring, and bite his opponent on the leg.

When the matches finished, Grandma would smile, playfully slap my thigh, and slide me to the floor. Up the stairs she'd go to see her daughter and have some tea. I was on my own to watch the women's roller derby. Forearms smashed into throats, solid belly punches, and handfuls of hair-pulls rivaled the men's wrestling action that Grandma loved. Skaters would be launched off the wood track into the stands, and you could count on at least one solid fistfight among the women athletes.

Only minutes into the carnage, she'd yell down to me, "Bobby! Bobby, come up here, stop looking at those cheeky legs, and come and get some cookies."

Grandma wouldn't let me watch too much of that show, those ladies' outfits were too *floozie* she'd say.

If I didn't respond, I guess I must have been looking at those short shorts and cheeky legs. Her next response would come from the other side of Grandma's smile.

"Shut that off and get up here now!"

There was no third request. Grandma's hands-on disciplinary policy waited for me if I delayed. Besides, I could never turn down those oatmeal raisin, saucer-sized gems served from the warming pan she'd pull out of the oven. It was clear that when we left her playroom, Grandma became the other one, the enforcer. Only her winks on Sunday spoke to what we had shared the day before.

Learning to Fight

The first time that I got beaten up and ran home crying happened on a Saturday. *The Fist, a* big kid from up the street who delighted in wrestling us to the ground and punching us, targeted me that day. He outweighed us all by at least ten pounds and knew how to use his fists. He'd taunt us before closing in for the kill.

Both my parents were home that day and I expected instant retribution against that older bully. I burst through the door, dramatically increasing the volume of my screams. I hoped Mom would bolt out the door, apron flying in the wind, grab that bully and shake him good. That was a major miscalculation on my part.

Mom, who had grown up with ten other siblings during the Depression in an Irish neighborhood in Brooklyn, had another way of looking at this. First, use your words, then your fists. Don't look for a fight, but don't run from one either. Get your shots in before your opponent clubs you. She made it clear that your mouth would definitely get you into trouble, but might also get you out of it. But if your words failed, never walk away when struck. Fight back. After all, that's what she did as a kid. Cowardice was unacceptable, but worse was taking a beating and crying about it later.

Mom called my dad over to begin my self-defense lessons. Dad took me out back, knelt down, and grabbed my shoulders and showed me how to stand, jab, block, and weave, and make a proper fist, thumbs tucked out not under your fingers. I never thought that he knew any of this. He was a quiet, gentle man and a proper office manager, well-dressed with a tie and leather briefcase. Dad had two weeks for vacation each year, and spent one week painting our house and the other taking us on car trips to Washington, D.C., the Blue Ridge Mountains or the Luray Caverns in Virginia. He was the patient man of few words, who with a cigar in hand, floated in an inner tube in our pool. He shouldn't have known much about fighting, but he did.

I was anxious to try out my newly acquired skills and vowed next time to stand my ground and not cry. My street was the main theatre of operation. We kids played on that asphalt, raced our bikes and ate there, learned about the birds and the bees and shared ice cream there, shot fireworks off from its curbs, and, yes, fought on that street.

My first encounter wasn't successful, but it was memorable. *The Fist* still prevailed, but when I gave him a wallop in the face, his surprise melted into more anger. Shortly thereafter, I picked myself up off the ground and wiped the blood from my mouth. I noticed that he was bleeding too. I went home, no tears, hair messed up, and shirt ripped, with dried blood on my mouth.

Well, it didn't take long for the word to get around that I had fought back. That didn't mean I got any more respect from the local hood. But I hoped that maybe next time he'd reconsider his choice of victim. It must have irked him that Carl, his younger brother, and I became good friends that fall, particularly after President Kennedy was shot. It turned out that Carl and I sat next to one another in Mr. Robinson's fifth grade class the day that our principal walked into the room to announce the assassination of President Kennedy. I snapped my pencil in half and threw it at the blackboard. Carl put his head down on his desk. After a few minutes of silence on our part, we looked at each other and vowed to hunt down the murderer and take his life.

Two days prior Mr. Robinson had hung up the autographed photo of JFK that my sister had been given for running the East Northport JFK Headquarters during the 1960 presidential campaign. I worked there a couple of Saturdays too, handing out pamphlets and buttons on the sidewalk in front of the campaign office. I felt proud to have my sister's signed photograph of Kennedy hanging behind my teacher's desk.

The other kids were crying or sitting in silence. A few jokers jostled in the back of the classroom. Not everyone loved Kennedy and some of the kids in class were more enthusiastic about the prospect of being dismissed soon, and starting Thanksgiving vacation early. But so many of us were in tears. Mr. Robinson, red-eyed, carefully framed that photo of JFK with black construction paper. He sat down in silence and put his head on his desk. Though I was shaken, above all, I was angry.

When *The Fist's* cronies would corner me on the playground, I'd try to remember the anger I felt that horrible day. I'd use that memory to help me stand up to them. They gave me plenty of practice. I got pretty good with my fists and learned to take a punch. Those after-school fights taught me to do that. Eventually I became the defender of my crowd. Although at times, I got carried away using my fists and physically bullied others too.

But the day I took on Willis, the older, rich kid who had a go-cart, who had beaten up my friend Deven, I understood why I learned to fight. Deven was one of several children who lived two houses down the street. His dad worked hard, but it seemed that they were always struggling. One Friday night his dad was killed in a car accident. We were all very sad for the family. And Deven should never have been made a target.

The rich kid had no idea what was coming his way. I challenged him on his front lawn, punched him in the face quite a bit, and took his punches well. He gave up the fight and ran into his house, slamming his screen door behind him and crying to his mom. I heard her shouting, "Look what they've done to you!"

Of course there was no *they*, it was just *I*.

Swollen lips and bloody noses signaled watershed moments in the lives of us kids on this street. And he had both. His mom yelled at me from their stoop, and threatened to call my parents. If she did, my mom never said anything to me about that.

After some time, fist fighting became a daily event for me. I'd schedule a fight with a kid named Stanley who was in my class. He was taller than I, with a proverbial crew cut, second generation English. Being Irish, I felt an ancestral obligation to try to thrash the Englander.

We fought daily for one month without an apparent winner. Each day we'd exit the school after the last bell, drop our books, square off, and box. We had both heard how each other's ethnicity was detested in our respective families and did our best for God, country, and our families' homelands. We'd land a few blows, sometimes to the face, which only would enrage the victim. Body blows were common, no kicking, biting or hair pulling. There was no honor in any of that. The fight would last a couple of minutes. We'd step back and agree that it was a draw, pick up our books, and head home.

When we got to the sixth grade we started to develop physically. Realizing that we could do serious damage to each other, we called a truce. That day, we were in the middle of a fight in early October, looked at one another wearily, got into the fighting stance when unexpectedly, he suggested that after the fight I come over to his house, get something to eat, and we could roll billiard balls at his lead soldiers. What a perfect way to end the years-old dispute, snacks and mowing down British lead soldiers! I suggested that we just go right then, and off we went, never to fight again.

We even had a time when we'd hang out in his home and listen to the latest Beatle songs. When I met his mom for the first time, she looked at him and said, "So, Stan, this is the lad you've been fighting? Do you want some milk? Maybe biscuits?"

Then I realized that our moms were the same; milk and cookies cured all ills. We weren't Irish or British, just two American kids who liked snacks.

Walking the Tracks

There were plenty of things we never told our folks. I'm sure that we weren't any different than they were when they were kids. Secrets, pinky swears, and cross-the-heart promises bonded us kids together. We understood that under withering interrogation by our parents there would be slips of the tongue and unintentional leaks. But walking the train tracks was something we all vowed to keep strictly confidential. These walks were an inviolate secret, never to be mentioned in school, to casual acquaintances, and absolutely never shared with any family member. If the topic ever came up in conversation at the dinner table, we promised to maintain silence and plead absolute and utter ignorance about what "those other kids" did on the Long Island Railroad tracks.

Most of my walking crew never had to deal with "the smile and deny" we had sworn to give to our parents. Their dads drove to work. But in my house I surely would because my dad had ridden the LIRR five days a week to Manhattan for decades. He certainly had heard plenty of stories about young kids getting sucked under trains while trying to put pennies on the tracks. The local newspapers reported on missing kids who were found days later in the brush along the solitary stretches of railroad lines we had in Huntington Township. They'd be found lifeless, either intact or chopped to pieces, blasted out of their clothes or just missing their sneakers. Anyway, we were way too smart to make those mistakes. Besides, our walking the tracks had loftier goals.

We walked the tracks weekdays on summer mornings after the commuter rush had subsided. It always started with us roaming the farm fields that bordered the tracks. Tired of investigating the same old farm field, we'd cross over to the tracks and walk along them heading east to Kings Park.

We'd be unrecognizable blurs if passengers in the speeding train cars had seen us. The few times that trains approached us as we walked the rails, we'd jump into the brush, crouch down and brace ourselves as it roared by, blasting fallen leaves, pebbles and dust up from the train bed into our hiding places. We 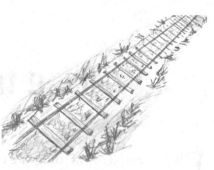 loved the whoosh of those iron tsunamis as they smashed through the air. The sweet stench of creosote-soaked railroad ties engulfed us. The shockwave of air and the roar of the train buzzed in our ears. Momentarily numbed and deafened, we'd walk in silence, reliving that moment. The smell of the pines, the hum of the cicadas, and the crunch of our footsteps on the large stone ballast of the rail bed surrounded us as we walked into the shadows of the Old Bridge Overpass. After screaming our names and whatever stupidity occurred to us into the darkness of the echoing vault, we sat in its quiet and coolness as cars thudded overhead. Down the tracks, stood the blackness of another overpass and past that, the Town Line Road trestle. This was the first adventure that had taken me this far from home and I feared that this one might be dangerous.

We headed down the tracks towards the abutments of the Pulaski Road Overpass near Richter's Orchard. The yak yak started about the giant nude woman that waited for us under that overpass that we called the Naked Lady Bridge. Now, I had never seen a nude woman before, but certainly wasn't opposed to seeing my first. The more experienced in our crowd, the older kids who led the way, acted as if she were their dear old friend. They enjoyed educating us, the uninitiated ones, about the details and accuracy of what we were about to behold.

She stood facing the tracks for all to see. Unabashedly, she displayed all. I'm sure she must have jolted awake sleepy commuters who happened to glance out their windows as their train sped under the bridge. There, on the train trestle's concrete support, an Amazon-sized naked woman stared unblinkingly out past me to the far side of the tracks.

Outlined in white paint with all of the significant details from the curls in her hair to her jumbo-sized toenails, the oversized, naked woman of the Pulaski Road Overpass luxuriated in the sultry shadows cast in the morning sun. The anonymous, well-studied artist, unquestionably experienced with a woman of this magnitude, depicted every significant detail, according to our esteemed mentors. We little kids just stood there and gawked, knowing we'd carry that image with us for the rest of the summer … or longer. Unlike our older compatriots, we eventually tired of her and wanted to get on to the more challenging stretch of our journey, crossing the train trestle that passed fifty feet above Town Line Road.

The trestle, an 1870s cross-braced structure, marked the border of a wild frontier that fascinated us kids. The county dumps, where we procured all kinds of treasures, spread out to the south of the trestle. Flocks of seagulls encircled its property where the incinerator's stacks belched blackish gray smoke several times a day. My Uncle Eddie worked there and he'd always let us kids in to scrounge around for goodies.

The sand works with its giant excavators bordered the north side of the tracks that crossed the trestle and continued the North Shore line through Kings Park. The end of the run was Judge's Hotel in Wading River. The big kids would sneak into the sand works at night and ride cardboard "sleds" down the sides of the sand hills to the pools of water that pockmarked the grounds. We *termites* weren't ever invited on those night runs.

Crossing the Town Line trestle weighed heavily on us runts. Though the older boys said that they had crossed it many times, they appeared more worried than seasoned scouts should have been. I could hear them debating which fate would be worse; slipping to their deaths or being caught in the middle of the trestle and having to decide to jump or be smashed to soupy pulp by the locomotive. They snickered when they made these comments in earshot of us little kids. They probably knew that there wouldn't be a train for a while. Just busting the horns of us *ankle biters* as the oldest of the group called us.

Foremost in my mind was not giving them the pleasure of making me turn back. *Just a walk like any other*, I tried to convince myself. I focused on all the details of our rail-walking; the collectible old whiskey bottles, flattened coins, and discarded sleeper spikes. I thought back on our storytelling, jokes and, of course, that naked Amazon.

Void of any undergrowth, the ballast apron led us to the trestle. The expanse of track and steel girders stretched over the road and made land in a clearing in the woods on the other side. The trestle seemed the length of a football field but probably extended less than forty feet. I thought of the movie *Bridge on the River Kwai* that my parents had taken me to see. All of us kids knew the theme song and we whistled it on the school playground, playing soldier, and even on our rail-walking outings. I distracted myself, thinking about that movie's importance to me and my family.

The British prisoners of war whistled it as they marched over the bridge that they had built for their Japanese captors. In the finale, saboteurs blew it up as the enemy's train crossed it. I was shocked by the end of the film when all the major English and American heroes died. At least the members of my family who served in World War II had faired better.

That war was always a presence in the things we kids discussed, played or watched in the movies. I could only imagine how real it still felt for my uncles who survived combat and did their best to meld back into society. Uncle Warren, a gifted automotive mechanic, photographer and general tinkerer, repaired cars in a local gas station after the war. He once shared with us how his plane was shot down over Burma. He and his crew had to fight their way out of the Burmese jungle, sometimes fighting hand to hand with the Japanese. Uncle Eddie worked at the local dumps, a political appointment from the Democratic Party for his loyalty and support. He had serviced planes in Europe for the Army. He walked with a permanent gimp due to an airfield accident. I only knew my Uncle Billy through my family's stories. He lived in California after serving in the Submarine Service. He suffered from trauma due to his time in the Pacific. I remember the discussion of how my mom and her siblings had to pool their money to ship his remains from San

Diego back to New York when he passed away. Thinking about all this distracted me as I crossed that trestle.

A few of our gang decided to hang back and wait for our return. Maybe they'd cross the next time. No one got razzed for being scared. We all were afraid. They promised to keep secret our crossing. We knew that they'd be gone before we got back.

The big kids led the way as we started to cross.

"Don't look down, keep your yaps shut, and walk down the middle of the railroad ties!"

We termites followed their orders and kept moving quietly. I didn't look down even though I was tempted to.

"Keep moving!"

The silver steel girders disappeared beneath us and the sleeper-railroad ties and rails before us seemed to float out into space. I did look off to the sides. It was amazing! It felt like we were floating up there.

"Move it, runts. Train's gonna be coming," one of the older kids growled.

I'm walking … I'm walking, I thought, and picked up my pace.

The big kids had already made it to the other side and stood off of the tracks near the woods. They watched us squirming inside as we gingerly stepped on the railroad ties.

"Get your fat butt moving, Hodum! Or it's splat for you!"

Crazy thing about it, they weren't just busting our balls. We could feel the trestle vibrating. A train couldn't be far away. The big kid wasn't joking this time.

I considered this advisement to be more than just motivational, so I moved my butt and did a duck-waddle quickstep along the greasy sleepers on the trestle. And I made it over. We all did and acted as if we had just walked home from school. We kids gathered near the sandpit's fence near the woods, joked, laughed, and bragged about how easy that was. *None of us were afraid*, we declared. We all knew *that* was a lie!

We moved along the tracks in the direction of the Kings Park train station. We slipped into the brush and trees as a train whistle sounded as it approached the trestle. The engineer must have seen us and wanted to make it clear to stay off the tracks. It roared by, shaking the ground beneath us. Most people never got this experience of feeling the weight, force, and roar of a diesel engine like that. We'd never forget it.

There were some empty lean-tos with bundles of clothes and rumpled up blankets along this stretch of tracks. One of the older kids ducked under one of the tarps. We yelled at him to get out of there, that the owner might come back and catch us. He dawdled around, trying to be cool, teasing us. He came out with some empty sardine cans. They had to belong to the hobos that my folks had told me about; dangerous men that lived in these isolated areas along the tracks. We halfheartedly broke some of the empty whiskey bottles on the tracks, talked about it getting late, and decided it was time to head home.

The trip back home was a reprise of a very memorable day. We carefully crossed the trestle, a little less nervously this time and followed the tracks past the dumps. We'd throw ballast stones at anything that moved in the brush or up in the trees. Occasionally, we'd chuck a stone at one another, eliciting plenty of laughs and some cursing. Of course, we bid our fond adieus to the naked Amazon under the Pulaski Road Overpass. It started to get late, so we double-stepped our way along the tracks, through the fields of potatoes and cauliflower to the front doors of our homes that stood silently waiting for us.

That night my folks asked me how my day was. I hesitated. Some days weren't very special, but others were just like this one, truly worth remembering. Maybe someday I'd tell someone about today. But not tonight.

I answered, "Well … nothing special, just messing around."

Saturdays at the Movies

Many of our parents had grown up in exotic places like Brooklyn, Queens, and a lordly sounding locale, The Bronx. Trollies, metro buses, and subways crisscrossed their childhood stomping grounds. They measured their worlds by city blocks, managing trips to school, shopping, and entertainment with aplomb. Apparently this autonomy and independence at an early age didn't come without a price. As they told us, all of them had studied in "The School of Hard Knocks." There, they assured us that they had learned lessons which we knew nothing about and might never learn in this suburban world of potato fields and multi-story homes on half-acre plots. Frankly, that sounded fine to me. And if I didn't have to go to *that* school, I'd sure be happy.

So, early on, they let us try out our wings and scrape our knuckles in the world that waited for us in our lives too. We had permission to walk the mile and a half uptown to Hewitt Square and its shops. We'd get our obligatory crew cuts at the German barber shop, seventy-five cents for the haircut and twenty-five cent tip for Mr. Hans who always did the children's haircuts. All the while, we kept our eyes open for those hard knocks.

We all had chores to do at home. Most of us got allowances and were allowed to spend our fortunes on simple pleasures. The Five and Dime store with those creaky wood floors had trinkets, balsa wood planes with red propellers powered by rubber bands, bouncy balls, and plastic paratroopers with wide, colorful parachutes. The soda fountain next door had comic books, ice cream sundaes, and plenty of candy.

We loved those walks, the chats and debates, and the sense of autonomy, but the double feature at the local movies was the most impactful of those trips uptown. That movie house became another locale where we played and grew up. Off we'd go with the ticket price in our pockets, to be forever changed by what we saw on the screen and our camaraderie-flavored hijinks in the shadows of our movie house. Weeks of fantasies and playtime reenactments spiraled off all those B-movies. We chomped down hard on those experiences.

Our Saturday morning movie ritual, which included a full-length film with cartoons, started at 11:30 in the morning and ran until 2 o'clock in the afternoon. We'd walk up to the Larkfield Movie House, the *Itch*, known for its infrequently vacuumed carpets, musty dust-encrusted wall curtains, and the sharply angled, shadowy balcony. We'd tromp up what we kids named the *Olde Indian Trail,* a dirt path that wound around centennial trees along Pulaski Road. We passed the housing developments on the left and the remaining farmhouses on the right, which were bordered by the woods and the cultivated fields. The pony farm and its stable were across the street from the Babe Ruth Baseball Field, near the corner of Pulaski and Larkfield Roads. We hurried past the library for fear of being spotted anywhere near it. The East Northport Firehouse, where we'd go to the annual Firemen's Fair, was on the left. We'd scan the storefront windows that might have some novelty or sports paraphernalia hidden behind appliances or clothing. But we never seriously wavered from our destination and headed straight to the doors of the cinema. Always early, the doors were invariably locked, but we'd pull on them anyway.

Studying the movie posters that announced the day's shows, we'd argue over which one looked the best and discuss whether we'd seen it already. Reruns were frequent, but it just didn't matter. This was the premiere outing for us kids. Always with our friends, we treated ourselves to popcorn or a box of Good & Plenty and screamed when the lights went out. We'd spot our rivals in the audience and throw the occasional piece of candy their way, and always shout witticisms at the screen. It was like being at school without any teachers.

The films were of four genres. Science fiction was the most preferred, yet easiest to criticize. War movies were the most revered, since we imagined ourselves in the starring roles, fighting alongside our uncles or dads who had shared their war stories with us. We enjoyed westerns that had inordinate amounts of shootouts as well as movies that highlighted the exploits of Hercules, Sinbad or Jason and his Argonauts. These had bloodless sword fights and actresses in flowing gowns, which revealed just enough to solicit whistles and more than one vulgar comment. Horror films were the most secretly feared because all of us would return home to sleep alone.

If we were lucky these genres would be combined, pitting cowboys against dinosaurs, gorilla-like space creatures kidnapping scantily clothed Earth women, and battlefields of tanks that were immolated by alien death rays. The rare comedy, Charlie Chan mysteries, Abbott and Costello adventures or the Three Stooges slapstick were always appreciated.

The cinema had two long aisles, which sloped to the screen that was suspended above a stage, which doubled as a venue for rock and roll bands in the early fifties. The ticket booth was the point of no return. We handed over our allowance for one ticket, and in we went. The usher, dressed in a uniform, fidgeted with his flashlight. The candy concession stood near the bathrooms. We'd run straight ahead and sit on the right side, our exclusive section. The stairs to the balcony were off to the left.

Saturday matinees were unquestionably a madhouse. This was obvious in the scowl of the usher who feigned interest in seating us. He was an older gentleman who gave the same instructions to us every Saturday; be quiet during the movie, no feet on the seats in front of you, no throwing things. We discounted all of this the moment the lights went out. If things got particularly ugly, he'd make a foray into the crowd, singling out the culprits with the beam of his flashlight and gesture threateningly. On the rare occasion, he'd pull someone out and remove them from the cinema. If he had had his preference, he would have locked the cage and let us beasts go at it. At times, frustrated with us little monsters, he'd just go sit at the concession stand and read his newspaper. Understand that it wasn't that we didn't watch the films. There were moments of silence and awe. All of us were certainly committed moviegoers, but the constant movement and hum of conversations and laughter forced most of us to become excellent lip readers.

Of course those in the balcony seemed to always be quiet. Reserved exclusively for couples that passed muster as being at least in junior high school, the balcony was terra incognita for us fans of the Saturday matinee. The occasional couple who ventured to the matinee glowered at us when we whispered about them as they made their way up to their shadowy domain. We heard all kinds of stories about what happened up there and who went up with what girl. We runts couldn't quite understand the attraction. Sitting alone with a girl and without the boys was unthinkable.

Most of the big kids wouldn't be there with their dates on late Saturday mornings anyway. They worked at the A & P supermarket near the Northport train station or Bohacks in Hewitt Square, unboxing canned goods, sifting through perishable vegetables and bagging freshly baked bread and rolls for customers in the bakery. Others worked at the local Carvel. They'd be polite to us at work, but we knew not to cross their paths at the movies. Having to say hundreds of forced *You're welcomes* left them surly and ready to kick butt.

One time a group of us snuck up the balcony's stairs to see what was going on up there. The couples were spread out around the balcony; some hidden in the back corners, their faces buried in one another's, others closer together on group dates. A group of older boys sat in the front row behind the railing. They had been the ones that had been peppering us kids with hard candy and had used rubber bands to shoot paperclips at the screen that day.

Those older high school kids with a *What-are-you-doing-up-here* glare made it clear that we had to sit downstairs. Scowling, they flexed their arms, cracked their knuckles, and slowly moved toward us. They knew that they were subject to the usher's rules just like us, but we had invaded their territory and they made their message clear, *Termites, get downstairs!* With shoulders rolled and heads down, muttering an obligatory apology, we snaked back down the stairs, stalling at the bottom to give the impression to our friends that we'd been up there hanging with the big kids.

We hesitated to go to the restroom during intermission because the big kids picked on squirts like us. They loved to comb their greased back hair and stare at themselves in the mirrors. Desperate, we'd slip into a stall to take care of our business and hope to sneak out unscathed. Most of us just held it until after the last show and we'd go outside in the alley.

We tried our best not to offend the *knighted ones,* though that was tough given our penchant for pushing the envelope. When they took offense, we paid the price with the occasional headlock and knuckle-grating on our noggins. Ill-intentioned or in jest, they clearly marked their territory and embarrassed us with those public head-raspings.

Although we whined initially about our sore heads, ultimately it was a source of pride. Everyone knew that we had faced the dragon and had gotten singed, but survived just like some of our cinematic heroes.

Hanging Out with Cousin Dennis

Whenever Mom went over to see her parents in Huntington, I would go along. Aunt Jessie and her son, my cousin Dennis, lived with my grandparents. The few words I grasped from hushed conversations highlighted how Grandpa Cross' generosity had saved them. Once, while up in Dennis' room, away from the adult prattle, I saw a picture of him and his mom on his dresser. I asked him where his dad was. He said that one day he went away. No other words about that ever passed between us.

Dennis, at sixteen, wore a black leather jacket, tight jeans and slicked-back greasy hair and liked to hang out with the *hoods* at the local bowling alley or soda shop. Often in trouble in his high school, he'd refuse haircuts, sneak out when grounded, and come home late. Grandpa used his stern countenance and strong backhand to keep my rule-breaking cousin in line. It didn't always work. When the shouting matches with Pops, as he called Grandpa, boiled over, my mom would get a call. Dennis didn't like dealing with his Aunt Mary, the enforcer, who looked him in the eye, and with a strong point of her finger, made it clear that she would take no prisoners.

Their's was the most peculiar love-hate relationship. Frequently exasperated by the late night phone calls and the face-to-face conflicts my mom endured, she'd comment how she loved him, but sometimes wanted to slap him silly. Of course, that never happened, but she did verbally grab him by the collar more than once. She'd pull Dennis by the proverbial ear to the barbershop, insist that he bathe, and often calmed down her dad and mom who threatened to turn him out on the street. But often, I saw her slip money into his pocket.

He'd give her a kiss on the cheek, and whisper, "Thanks, Aunt Mary."

"Use it well," she'd reply.

Privy to all the anger, sorrow, and frustration he caused, I still cared very much for my cousin. I looked forward to seeing him, though sometimes being with him felt like walking blindfolded and barefoot over a floor covered with broken glass.

One Saturday Grandma forced Dennis to "babysit" me while she, Aunt Jessie, and my mom had their tea and caught up on the goings-on in the ever-growing and not always amicable Cross family. Grandpa John, who by then was hard of hearing, had rigged up a chair-mounted speaker right next to his right ear, so he could watch *and* hear the Yankees play, which he faithfully did while chain-smoking stogies in his easy chair. There was always a bluish-gray cloud around the center of the room where he had the TV, his smoking stand, and comfy, worn chair.

Well, after some discussion that day with Grandma, Dennis was given permission to go out, but had to take me along. He was given strict instructions to keep an eye on me, not to see his "hoodlum friends", and definitely not to smoke in front of me. He promised, kissing the women at the table, and patting Grandpa John's bald head as we headed for the door. That was his goodbye to the family's diehard Yankee fan. Before his hand was on the doorknob, Grandpa growled, his finger pointing at my cousin, "Dennisss ... !"

My cousin froze and turned to this frail man who had tried his best to fill his father's shoes. He looked directly at the long, gnarled finger held unflinchingly in the air that Grandpa pointed at Dennis' face.

He replied sheepishly, "Yes, Pops."

Their eyes still locked, Dennis nodded, and we headed out to the street.

We walked in silence for awhile. That encounter shocked me. I knew Grandpa had always been a man to be reckoned with and never crossed. My mom had told me stories of him as an overseer on dairy farms in Greenpoint, Brooklyn when she was a kid. He'd lay a gun down on the kitchen table as he had his morning coffee, the gun he took to work everyday, six days a week to the farms out in the sticks of Greenpoint. The kids feared him and only Mom's brother Billy, my long-lost uncle who lived out in California, battled with him, sometimes resorting to fisticuffs. Grandpa, hard as seasoned wood, never lost.

Dennis probably discovered that side of Grandpa, while I just knew him as the quiet, paterfamilias who when in the mood told us some wonderful yarns about the leprechauns, his beloved *Little People*. He told us how John Ryan, his great-grandfather on the maternal side of the Cross family history, dug his way out of paupers' prison with a spoon that he had pilfered from some inn in County Cork. He was a stowaway who jumped ship and swam ashore to Staten Island in the early 1790s. His wanderings brought him to Greenpoint, Brooklyn. It was his son, Edward Ryan who fought at the first Battle of Bull Run and had his middle finger shot off by "a Confederate S.O.B." as my Grandpa John liked to call the Rebel marksman. Edward's daughter, Bridgett Ryan, was my grandpa's mom and the wife of Edward Cross, whose father, Joseph Cross, was born in Ireland. Grandpa John's stories seemed to blur the distinction between the Ryan and Cross families and confused me at times, but it didn't really matter because Grandpa John's tales were so entertaining.

The moment we hit the street Dennis unrolled the pack of "cigs" from the sleeve of his T-shirt and lit up.

"Not a word," he said, pointing a finger in my face.

Off to the soda shop we went. His instructions to me were clear: keep my mouth shut, stand away from the group and never, under any circumstances, say that I knew him.

I agreed.

His gang, all dressed the same as he, liked to do the slow, open-palm drag-slap to greet one another. The slower the drag and the harder the slap, the more alpha male coolness one had.

"How's it hanging, Denny boy?"

That was something only the blonde wearing the tight sweater and jeans could call him. And, yes, tight jeans were for hoods, the in-crowd, and chinos, for the rest of us dweebs.

I sat on the side of the soda shop's front porch as they all cursed up a storm and joked around. One guy, who must have been the leader, squeezed his arm around some girl there, and looked over at me.

"Hey kid, what are you doing here? Waiting for a bus?" he said as he spat over at me.

Dennis was quiet.

The gang erupted in laughter.

Dennis looked at me with a "keep-your-mouth-shut" glare.

"Yeah, you, you little turd, what the hell are you doing here? Beat it!"

I stood up, went over towards the group, and looked him in the eye, and said, "I'm here with my cousin Dennis who's babysitting me, so you better not bother me or he's going to kick your butt!"

This might have worked on a grammar school playground, but not here.

The leader grabbed me by the arm and pulled me over to the middle of the group. "You little shit, I'm going to kick your ..."

At that point, Dennis reached over, grabbed this guy's arm and said, "That's not going to happen! He's my cousin, and even for a little turd like him, he's got horns, so leave him alone!"

My cousin must have commanded respect here, because the bully let me go, said something about how I should go play in traffic, spat, turned, and kissed his girlfriend.

Everybody laughed, Dennis winked at me and I sat back down, kicking the dirt. I mulled over his order, "Not a word!"

I honored that request for the rest of the day. They all had Cokes, told jokes, petted the girls in the crowd who squealed, and then snuggled tighter to the guys who had gotten handsy with them. I heard it all that day; boss cars, who was or wasn't righteous, those fag teachers they had, and punks who they punched in the face in the cafeteria or beat up after school, and tales of who they "copped feels" from or with whom they went "all the way".

They all smoked, some pulled cigs from behind their ears, and couples passed smokes between themselves. They grubbed lights when it was time for a fresh smoke. After grinding their cig butts under their Beatle boot heels on the planks of the wood porch, the guys spat out onto the dirt of the parking spaces in front of the private home that doubled as a soda shop.

Dennis left this crew first, saying he had to get me home. Gang handshakes, "See ya, man" all around, hugs from some of the girls, some ranks from the guy I pissed off earlier, my cousin gave my foot a gentle kick to signal our moving on. Some girl said to me, "Hey, come back when you're older." I turned red, and followed Dennis out to the road.

Out of earshot of his posse, he pointed out, "You did pretty good today. At least you didn't get beat up."

He brushed the back of my head as we walked along, saying, "It was okay with you there today. You were cool. Sounds like Marlene likes you ... But don't take that too seriously, she likes everybody."

He laughed as we neared home.

Right before we got to the door, he pulled me back, and looked hard at me.

"Not a word, right? Not a word."

He was asking me to be "righteous".

"Nope, not a word," I said.

I'd make something up about going for a walk to a playground. The adults didn't ask much except whether I had had fun. Of course I did, I'd tell them. After all, I was with my cousin Dennis.

After that day, I didn't see Dennis much. I overheard that he was working on weekends. Sometimes at Easter or for the Fourth of July, we'd all get together. My mom made a point of taking me and my sister to his high school graduation. Aunt Jessie, wearing a new dress, looking so proud, my grandparents, Mom, Fran and I sat near the stage and cheered when Dennis' name was called. He sauntered up to the principal, took the diploma, turned and faced the audience, thrusting his arms over his head. His friends' cheers and whistles came from the back of the crowd.

My mom looked down, and directed my way a very audible, "Whew! Finally got him through!"

I looked over and she was crying.

Grandpa John's Best Tall Tale

The Irish side of my family, harder hit by the Depression and with only a few books at home, were the impromptu singers, storytellers, and spinners of the fantastical and implausible. During meal taking, they walked the ever-shifting line between truth and hyperbole, and fact and fantasy in their depictions of the weeks' events at their home's table.

Grandpa John Cross was my link to that world. This hardened sentinel sat at our table for Sunday dinners, his hot cigar ashes burning holes in his sweaters. A firm believer in cleaning his plate before conversation, the stories would flow only after his fork and knife came to rest. He'd speak of his childhood adventures on Delancey Street, going to work with a revolver tucked in his shirt, his grandfather's loss of his middle finger at Bull Run and the paterfamilias of the Cross-Ryan family history who dug his way out of pauper's prison with a spoon back in County Cork. Grandpa John was the king of storytellers and our family's sage.

This overseer of dairy farms in Greenpoint, Brooklyn, hard-handed disciplinarian of the Cross brood, and guardian of his great grandfather's Irish heritage and shillelagh, when he took a break from his newspaper and removed the smoldering cigar from his mouth, drew tales in the air.

And this story was his most memorable one.

My great-great-great-grandfather on the maternal side, John Ryan, jumped ship into the Hudson River in 1791 and set the example for us to follow: never be afraid to get wet, strike out on your own when needed, and always keep one coin tucked deep in your pocket. The fact that he dug his way out of a pauper's prison in County Cork with a spoon he had stolen was only part of the Cross-Ryan family history. The litany of misfortunes that could befall you if you left home without a coin in your pocket was a Cross family standard. And then there were his tales of leprechauns.

The greatest of tales involved John Ryan, the family patriarch who mistakenly wore his finest, new shoes while shepherding a flock of sheep after Mass one foggy, County Cork Sunday morning. As the tale goes, he heard a rustling behind some bushes at the foot of a hillock, and snuck down to discover that there in the hollow, was a little person, crouched over and stitching up the sole of his worn-out boot.

Well, the young John pounced on him and held him tightly, making him swear that he'd reveal his lair and surrender his pot of gold. The little man agreed and suddenly the hollow beneath them opened up into a gaping hole that led down into a cave. John grabbed the little man's hand and down they went to the bottom of the pit where the pot of gold stood glistening and awaiting its new master.

Of course, my grandpa enlivened the tale with dialogue and a brogue that got heavier as the story progressed.

"And what would you have me do, young John?" asked the little man.

"I'd be taking your gold, ya know," he said.

"Well, I give you freely my gold, John, as much as you can carry out of my lair."

John reached down and began to fill his pockets with gold coins, stuffing them in as deeply as he could, pushing hard on the inside pockets that were worn and old. When John was done, he thanked the leprechaun and reminded him that there would be no tricks that day, and he began climbing up to the light of day.

Suddenly, the ground started rumbling and the rocks shifted. John hurried up to the sunlight as the hole began to close around him. The rocks and dirt began to tighten about him as he forced himself through the opening, fraying his pants and ripping his pockets. As John pushed his head

into the morning air, the hole was almost solid ground, and with the greatest of efforts, he pulled himself out, losing his left shoe to the closing hole that became the solid landscape of early morning. John lay on his back, winded.

And in the sun of that morning he knew that one of County Cork's finest leprechauns had outwitted him. John thrust his hand down in his pocket, and found but one gold coin. His left foot laid bare, his big toe poking out of his torn sock, his left shoe lost to the darkness of the leprechaun's lair.

John stood up, brushed himself off, gathered the sheep, and returned home. When he shared his story and showed his bare foot to his parents, John promptly got a thrashing for having lost that shoe. But he said nothing of the gold coin to his parents.

As Grandpa would continue, it was this John Ryan who stowed away to New York, jumped ship, and swam the waters of the Hudson River, and with a single coin, started a new life in America. John's son Edward, who lost his middle finger of his right hand to a Confederate Minie ball at the battle of Bull Run, sired Bridgett who married Edward Cross. It was Edward Cross' son, John Francis, who oversaw dairy farms in Greenpoint with a pistol tucked into his trousers. He married Louise Haupert, the daughter of a German dairy farmer. John Francis Cross, the cigar smoking teller of tall tales and Louise Haupert Cross, the stoic wrestling fanatic, sat at our dinner table every Sunday.

It was John Ryan's shillelagh that I'd see in the corner of Grandpa's living room. I came to appreciate through those stories how deep my family's roots were. They gave me a sense of belonging to something so much bigger than my life in East Northport. This faceless relative tied us all together, when almost two centuries ago, he left home to find another.

Happy Hooligan

My mom's side of the family was less enigmatic than my dad's. He rarely spoke of his childhood and family, but there were those moments when our coaxing paid off and we'd be treated to memorable and unexpected stories of his exploits as a child and his family's life in Brooklyn. Aunt Mae, his older sister, was often present during those moments when her baby brother opened up and dared to remember.

As far as I knew, she was the oldest survivor of the original Hodums. I had never met any of Dad's other siblings, never knew his mom, Elizabeth Kammerer, the pianist who spoke her native German and French with her children. Dad's father, Herman Hodum, the Bavarian butcher lived with his family on 256 Colvert Street in Brooklyn. The Kammerer family left Germany in 1873 after the Franco-Prussian War. The Hodums passed through Ellis Island in 1880.

My dad, born in 1908, attended an all-German primary school. German was the lingua franca in the Hodum household until the outbreak of World War I. Many who lived in the German section of Brooklyn stopped speaking their native language completely. The moment war was declared against Germany, all of the street names and restaurants or businesses in the Fatherland's language were changed to English with exclusively American themes.

All the Hodums were English speakers, but just like the typical immigrant experience, the children were more proficient than their parents. As Aunt Mae had told us, my Grandma Elizabeth continued to speak French and German. She was born in the Alsace Lorraine, a bilingual region where France and Germany faced off, sharing languages, commerce, and a long history of conflict. Herman spoke his childhood language at home. Aunt Jules, Uncles Arthur and George, Great Aunt Tata, who played the zither when she visited them, were known to me through stories and the few photos that my dad and Aunt Mae had.

The Dutch German side gifted books to family for Christmas and birthdays. Reading out loud to one another was a Sunday afternoon pastime in their Colvert Street home in Brooklyn. My father and Aunt Mae ended those evenings with violin and piano duets.

When Aunt Mae announced during one of her visits to us that the kids in their old neighborhood in Brooklyn called her little brother *Happy Hooligan*, she must have been trying to defuse a situation that my bad behavior had created either at school or during her visit. I can't recall the transgression, but Aunt Mae had always run interference between my confession of some act of minor terrorism and the impending wacking that lurked around the corner.

My confessions never came willingly, but were preceded by either a phone call or a note from my teacher. In the more severe cases, the letterhead of the Principal of Fifth Avenue Elementary School would be waved at me. I actually liked my principal, a calm, stout, meticulously groomed man who I got to know better than I should have over the course of the third, fourth and fifth grades.

Anyway, Dad just smiled when his nickname was revealed at the dinner table that night. He pulled back from his serious Dutch-German poker face that let me know that I should have behaved better in school. But generally, Dad was a mild-mannered Dutchman. Yes, the family was proud of their German heritage, but "Hodum" wasn't a German surname. Seems that the Hodums originated somewhere in Holland in the distant past. Our family's origin didn't matter much that night. And Aunt Mae's Happy Hooligan story was the perfect diversion from my impending scolding.

Well, my dad, Happy Hooligan, was quite a celebrity among the kids and families on the block. Since his father, Herman, owned the local butcher shop, the Hodums were known by German Americans in the surrounding neighborhoods. Dad, the cheery delivery boy and frequent visitor to many homes that had scheduled daily meat deliveries, was known as Happy Hooligan. My dad was the kid who ran, not walked, his deliveries to his father's customers' homes. So this smiling, local kid who sprinted the streets of the community got the name of a goofy character from the comic section of the Sunday newspaper.

By Aunt Mae's accounts, Dad reveled in this moniker and local fame. Since he got a salary of twenty-five cents a week, he was the only kid to have an expense account in the local candy store. Happy Hooligan was generous with his fortune and treated his buddies to candy once a week.

Prompted by his older sister, my dad shared his exploits as the youngest patron of the candy store who would settle his account at the end of each week. Turns out that a rolled-up newspaper cone of assorted candy cost five cents. He'd get one cone-full and he and his sweet-toothed cronies would spend the afternoon eating out of this enormous dunce cap-like candy bag. When Dad told the story, I could actually taste the candy and hear the newspaper being rolled up into a cone.

After settling his candy account on Friday, he'd put a dime away for the movies and save the rest. Going to the movies cost a nickel back then. An organist provided the soundtrack to those black and white silent films, apparently playing the same musical runs and flourishes for all the films. Kids back then were as raucous as we were at the movies.

There was no concession stand, at least not where Dad went to the movies. Each moviegoer could access the individual treat dispenser on the back of the seat in front of him. Insert a penny and turn the turnstile handle and you'd get a handful of treats all movie-long or at least as long as your pennies held out. Dad, by all accounts, always had a pocketful of change.

Dad won medals for his record-setting runs on the track team at Franklin K. Lane High School and still had the medals from his high school alma mater to prove it. When he entered the job market, he got a job as a *runner* for Socony Mobil Oil. The butcher's delivery boy became an office dispatcher, running the streets of Manhattan. His swift feet and computation skills later served him well when he was promoted from "runner" to accountant, and finally to the General Office Manager in Manhattan for his beloved Mobil Oil.

As a kid, I would see Dad sitting at his desk with yellow, legal-sized pads of paper doing calculations in pencil. I remember looking over his shoulders as he did his "computations" as he called them. My brother inherited that mathematical ability.

Dad liked to spend his money on good cigars and new cars. He bought the first car in the Hodum family, a Model-T Ford, when he advanced from runner to accountant for Mobil. He owned a Dodge, a Studebaker, and several Chevys. We had a two-door, light blue '62 Chevy Impala. He liked to buy a new car every three years. Some years, he'd just show up driving a new car, our old tried and true model gone forever. But sometimes, Mom would remind him that it might be time to visit the local dealership. He never had to be reminded twice.

By his own account, Dad started smoking when he was twelve. He'd sneak out to the outhouse in his backyard on Colvert Street and light up. He'd blow the smoke through the crescent moon cut out of the outhouse door. His dad smoked, so Happy Hooligan would raid his dad's cigar box that was kept on his father's smoking stand. My dad kept this antique in the living room next to his reclining chair in our house.

One Saturday, I showed some interest in smoking one of his cigars. He took me out back and had me take a puff from his. I choked and threw up on the spot. I never requested that again. He did the same with me when I asked for a taste of beer. I stuck with 7-Up.

But, inquiries about me being a smoker were commonplace. My teachers smelled cigar smoke on my clothes, and our dentist, Dr. Hetherwood, with a buzzing drill in hand, frequently had his face in mine. He cautioned me more than once against smoking stogies before coming in for my frequent appointments to fill cavities.

I may not have been blessed with the Hodum family's mathematics acumen, nor acquired a taste for stogies, but I certainly did inherit the Hodum sweet tooth.

Sandlot Baseball
and Parades

You wouldn't have known that we frumpy, grass-stained, dirt-caked kids were actually Baseball Hall of Famers. At least in our own minds, we distinguished ourselves in our weekly summertime sandlot baseball games. Those hot summer mornings when the folks went off to work, we'd gather in an open lot that the developer of our neighborhood had ceded to the township. Though never used by the adults or the municipality, that dirt lot was where we cut our teeth playing baseball.

We never bothered scaling the locked chainlink gate that led to our sandlot ballpark off of Kenilworth Drive. We'd sneak through neighbors' yards to access a barren, dirt field, encircled by the backyards of several of the homes in our neighborhood. We'd drag our bats along the dirt to outline the baselines and scuff out the bases in the dry soil, transforming that dirt field into our own baseball stadium,. There were no spectators, just late arrivals who waited to get subbed in, no hawkers selling peanuts and soda, no dugouts or backstops, and, above all, no adults. On this turf, we didn't have to be our polite, non-cussing selves who our parents knew most of the time.

Big kids mingled with us little *slugs* in day-long games where everyone played and said "Good game" to one another before going home to dinner. Whether we were picked first or last, we younger ones felt knighted when they chose us to be on their team. Nobody got bullied for being small, chubby, slow or less capable. If you didn't have a mitt, someone always brought extras, bats were plentiful, and everybody got a cheer when they did well, a "too bad" if they whiffed, and firm pats on the back for the losers as we all headed home after the last inning.

With no umpire to razz, we all called the game as we saw it. And although someone almost always disagreed with our calls, no individual imposed his rulings, and fairness and shared decision making seemed to rule most of our games. The disgruntled player who might throw a fit and threaten to leave was answered with cold-eyed stares and a chorus of *Ahh ...Go ahead.* That typically quieted the disgruntled one. These "big-kid little-kid" baseball collaborations were free of the crap we runts received at the hands of our former older teammates the rest of the year. I guess baseball was the great equalizer, the common thread that drew all of us together.

I'd regale my family at dinner time with the day's exploits, recounting our lunges and one-handed catches and how we clubbed the ball out of the park. Tales of our diving acrobatics or how we cracked line drives past shortstops, those sizzling hits that kicked up tufts of dust that made birds fall out of trees, broke the monotony of my parents' workday banter at our dinner table. Between the pass-the-potatoes background hum, my stories of how dogs howled at our home-runs drew some attention at meal time.

One day we desperately needed a ball to finish that afternoon's game. The old one we had been playing with had its threads split and the cowhide flayed open. Since no ump could throw in a new ball, the big kids talked of calling the game unless someone could procure one. My team was actually winning that day, so I was particularly keen on solving this problem. Besides, this could be my chance to be in the spotlight, the hero of the day, if I could produce a ball, especially a new ball.

I remembered one at home that had never seen the inside of a catcher's glove, never bounced along the infield, certainly never suffered the whack of a well-aimed bat. Yes, I knew where that one was! So, I ran home, went upstairs to my parent's bedroom, and took Dad's autographed baseball with the signatures of the 1957 Yankees off his desk. I proudly carried the unscathed ball out to my teammates. Their resounding cries of *Play ball!* cheered me on, and off we went to finish our game.

None of the kids seemed to notice the names scratched over the ball that we smacked around for several innings. I went home victorious with that ball in hand, though grass-stained and its signatures smeared. Dad didn't get home from the city until seven o'clock, so I had time to stealthily place the ball back exactly where I found it.

Before dinner Dad went up to change and wash up.

That's when I was summoned upstairs,

"Bob, I need to see you here ... right now!"

Dad was a gentle, quiet man who usually stepped away from any direct participation in my frequent scoldings. He'd just give me *the look*, that either melted the polar ice caps or expressed a head-shaking incredulity, *Really? You've got to be kidding?* But this offense might just merit something else.

I had convinced myself that *that* baseball didn't mean much to Dad. Yes, he enjoyed watching his games on Saturdays and chatting about the outcomes with Uncle Warren and my older brother. I'd listen and realized how little I knew about the game. But he never talked about that ball. Besides, the baseball sat so casually on his desk, almost totally ignored, and certainly waited anxiously to be noticed and used. He kept silent about the circumstances of acquiring it. Though I did know its origin story, Dad never spoke of it.

Before moving out to East Northport, in our old house in Glen Cove, Dad was friends with a blond haired, lanky neighbor who everybody called Whitey. I remembered playing with his children, all fair-haired just like their dad. He'd stop down once in a while, chat with Dad, and pitch underhand to us kids. I remember how he'd let us all get hits off of him. Well, our up-the-hill neighbor was Whitey Ford, the star pitcher for the New York Yankees. He had given the autographed ball with all the players of the '57 team to my dad.

I slogged up the stairs to face the music. Dad was at his desk. He turned to me and held out the ball.

"Well, tell me how this happened."

I told him how we needed a baseball, how the old one had its guts hanging out and how his looked like a good one, and how without it we'd never have finished today's game. And, oh by the way, Dad, my team won!

He sighed and told me not to ever do that again, that it'd be mine someday, and then I could do whatever I wanted with it.

"Really sorry, Dad. I won't do *that* again."

He smiled, put his hand on my shoulder, gave me a hug, and we went downstairs for supper.

Sandlot baseball was a small, comfortable world where we competed with well-known and friendly kids from our neighborhood. How I loved our summer sandlot games, but some kids started talking about another, bigger venue, Little League. So I decided to try it. But I soon discovered that playing on a team in our town's local baseball league had little to do with my sandlot experiences. Don't get me wrong, I enjoyed dressing up in those uniforms with their colorful hats and matching socks, looking like a real baseball player. It was fun folding those crisp, new visors down the middle and messing up those puffy pants with grass stains, but playing in an organized league just wasn't the same.

The tryouts when everybody watched me field grounders and pop flies intimidated me. After missing a few and hearing some groans from the sidelines, I started to feel that I just wasn't good enough. How could this be? Playing sandlot baseball made me feel like an all-star. But in Little League I worried about always having to measure up to an adult's standard I didn't really understand.

My coach started me as the catcher but that didn't work out. Instead of waiting for the pitch to reach me, I'd reach up and out for the ball and the batter would hit my catcher's mitt. I came to understand that that was the position where they'd put the slow, husky kid on the team. I felt like a human backstop. After that fiasco, I was relegated to playing left field. Not a lot of hits came my way out there. I dreaded it when the coaches would announce the lineup. *Hodum, left field* ... always seemed to be announced last. At times I felt like I was playing behind an invisible fence, distant, separate, and not equal.

I became the kid who couldn't meet the expectations of adult coaches or even my teammates and started to dread after-school practices. They expected us to be serious at practice, run the bases and field the coach's hits. There was no fun in any of that!

I tired of being the slow, fat kid who couldn't keep up. But no matter how bad I felt, there was a light at the end of that torturous tunnel, marching with my team in the Fourth of July parade.

We gathered in the morning at the King Kullen food market off of Clay Pitts Road. Of course, our uniforms were clean and pressed. I looked for my team's colors and got into formation. The coaches looked tired and surly that morning. I'm sure that they didn't appreciate playing drill sergeant on their morning off, but we kids were excited. Banners, flags, marching bands, and plenty of waving spectators and families that might call out our names! What's not to like? The high school marching band led the parade, followed by a contingent of veterans in uniform, the Daughters of the American Revolution and other civic groups followed the fire trucks that blasted their horns. I wasn't sitting on the curb for once, *watching* the parade. I was in it!

But there was also something else. Some of us kids had a secret mission.

The word had gotten got out the day before that a group of kids would be hiding in the trees with pea shooters along the parade route. Last year, they caught the uniformed kids by surprise and pelted them with chickpeas as they marched to the Babe Ruth field down by the library. But this year we kids would be ready for them. We had pockets full of well-chosen pebbles to pick off those snipers.

As we approached the end of the parade route, word spread to keep our eyes on the trees that lined this stretch of Larkfield Road. Sure enough we could see the kids hiding in the trees. I recognized some as my buddies from school who were out for some laughs. Expert marksmen with those pea shooters, they hit most of us. Our coaches, blissfully unaware of the flying, dried chickpeas, didn't notice our slight of hand as we started to respond in kind. Those knuckleheads in the trees didn't expect the fusillade of well-thrown, baseball-accurate pebbles that flew their way. In short order, they jumped down from the trees and retreated into the crowd.

Adults along the parade route reported our rock throwing to our coaches. We told them about the peashooters. Feigning shock and outrage, our coaches gave us a very public scolding for dishonoring the spirit of the day and sullying the reputation of our team. But out of earshot of the crowd, they complimented us on having fought back and praised the accuracy of our throws. That parade was definitely the most fun I had had that *entire* Little League season.

Shooting Rats

S hooting rats with slingshots in the garbage dump on the grounds of the Veteran Administration's Hospital in Northport was one of our entertainments on long summer days. Our hike took us through the farm fields off of Pulaski Road, over the train tracks to the woods north of Bellerose Avenue. Trails that wound through the woods led us to the outermost perimeter of the hospital's grounds. We'd go in groups of four or five, commando style, slipping through an opening in the V.A. fence. Our gang stealthily worked its way through the woods to a hill that overlooked the dump's mounds of medical waste and garbage.

The big kids used the large glass cat's eye marbles for the job. They filled the slings of their store-bought slingshots perfectly. Most days we hit more garbage than rats, but the infrequent thud against the engorged body of one of those beasts was worth the walk and the risk of getting caught. The rat would either flop on its side or jump screeching in the air and disappear over the crest of the dump. The occasional patrol car or garbage wagon that would appear at the perimeter of the hill of refuse interrupted our target practice. The few times that we were chased, we'd be deep in the woods before Security got within grabbing distance. We considered ourselves rugged frontiersmen, looking out for an unknown enemy as we walked through those woods. I thought that Davey Crockett surely must have done something like this on the olde frontier.

Bragging rights usually went to the marksmen among us who had metal slingshots and the strongest arms. Those were the "big kids" who threatened to leave us "termites" in the woods if we didn't do exactly what they said. During our hike, they'd tell us about bloodthirsty escapees from the V.A. Psych Ward who roamed these woods looking for food at sundown. We runts did our best to laugh off their stories but secretly hoped that if they abandoned us that we'd somehow figure out how to get home before the sun set. They'd try to keep a straight face while teasing us but would laugh after a while, punching us in our arms with a *Just-busting-them* look. We tried not to take it personally. After all, someday we'd be one of those older kids and rank on our younger compatriots.

Some of these guys had uncanny marksmanship skills. Each of their shots that impacted made a rat jump, rolling it into one of the heaps of medical waste at the dumps. Sometimes their marbles passed right through their fat bodies, kicking up a ketchup-like splatter. Other times they'd blow a leg off or hit a chubby rat belly. More often than not the marble ricocheted into the woods, digging up a whisk of dirt. That dumps was littered with marbles that never hit their marks.

Sometimes I'd get a turn with a metal slingshot, other times I'd bring my homemade one, fashioned out of the odd piece of tree branch that had a Y-shape. Rubber book straps could be tied or nailed to the arms of the Y, making a workable slingshot. I couldn't aim well with mine, and if I got off the lucky shot that would hit one, the rat would hop and scamper off, probably wondering what mosquito had just bitten him.

I never had a red-kill dot on my slingshot. Secretly, I felt relieved that I didn't. Dad warned me never to shoot at anyone. I promised, knowing that rats weren't part of that demographic, but I knew in my heart how disappointed he'd be if he knew what we were doing.

I stopped going out to the V.A. after I heard that one of the big kids got arrested. It never occurred to me that trespassing on federal land was far worse than blasting some disease-ridden rats. So, we *termites* focused on building things which turned out to be not only legal, but much more fun.

Hammers, Nails and the Dumps

f anything, we were junior builders. We pilfered hammers, nails, saws, and screwdrivers from our fathers' toolboxes and garages, and rarely returned them until the adults noticed their absence. One shout from an irate dad and the tools would magically reappear the next day, muddy of course, in their toolboxes or in a corner of the garage, but rarely in their proper places. We left shovels, rakes, and many a hammer out in the rain and were responsible for the premature rusting of almost all of our fathers' tools. But somehow that got overlooked when we took our dads out to see the creations that had cost the tools their youth. Dads were proud of their sons who could make something out of leftover lumber and refuse. Somehow the spilled paint on the garage floor, the tipped-over can of nails in the corner of the basement, and the missing 2x4s from their wood stock were irrelevant.

Granted, the dads always had to duck down to squeeze into our creations and crane their necks to see into their corners, but they always valued our work. Moms expressed their appreciation, but were more concerned about the rips in our clothing or the paint stains on our sneakers.

The treehouse was a certainty in our neighborhood. They were great for hiding out from the folks, telling stories, and for the occasional summer nap. They were defended at all costs and were not to be entered without invitation or expressed approval from the owner. We built our treehouses in the wild cherry trees that grew behind our homes. These trees were the easiest to climb and provided perches and level branches that made it easy to level flooring and nail it down. Walls would be extra planks or cardboard, roofs were optional but you had to have a rope to lift up cargo and personal treasures or even occasionally our pets.

We'd keep our comic books or baseball card collections there as well as food wrapped in this new stuff called aluminum foil, and, if you had one, a small thermos or cooler with drinks. An old blanket on the floor would complete the rustic décor. We'd visit one another's tree forts, always asking permission to enter before starting to scale the tree. Sharing building tips and studying the vantage points of our buddies' forts, we learned from one another. Sometimes we'd mount mock raids on one another, throwing wild cherries and crab apples during the attack. But most of the time we luxuriated in the tree forts' shade on hot summer days.

At the end of the day, we'd compare bruises and scrapes and stained fingers from the squished cherries. Besides having a great time, I came away with a sense of accomplishment. I'd step back and marvel at the great treehouse I had built. After, we'd be ready for hours of defending our forts from renegade Indians or a buddy's mock raiding party. Occasionally neighborhood girls would stop by and ask to climb up to inspect our work. Most of us proudly showed off our accomplishments.

Space ships and tanks were fashioned out of old cardboard boxes. Newspaper was used to fashion multi-winged paper airplanes and parachutes for our plastic soldiers. We'd use milk crates as chairs on the sets for our talk shows. Then we'd dress up and pretend to be Zachary the Ghoul, Mr. Green Jeans or Sky King. Soupy Sales was our hero whose show we watched on Saturday mornings while our parents slept in. We always imitated his awkward gestures, his slipping on bananas, and sang his silly ditties ... "Pachalafaka, pachalafaka, they whisper it all over Turkey. Pachalafaka, pachalafaka, it sounds so romantic and perky!"

Soapbox racers were our favorites and the ultimate achievement, requiring ball bearings, axels, rope, wheels, and recycled seats. Steering gear was made with rope and wood drag-brakes, nailed to the frames that we scraped along the ground to slow our speed. We'd get a lot of this stuff from the local dumps where my Uncle Eddie worked. He'd see us coming, open the gate, and wave us on to those glorious mountains of garbage.

The smell of decay called us to this treasure island of partially hidden gems. I liked the aroma of that place, and the taste of burned garbage and paper from the incinerator that lightly coated my throat. Old baby carriages, rickety chairs, planks of wood and other useful items jutted out from the piles of moldy grass clippings, cardboard boxes, broken toys, filthy stuffed animals and dolls, and tons of paper and food refuse. We'd climb up the slippery sides of this muck and grab what we could, pulling hard to dislodge these prizes. We'd rub our filthy hands on the legs of our pants and move on to the next pile.

If we found baby carriages or broken wagons with functioning wheels, we'd fill them with our other discoveries and take turns pushing their waddling carcasses towards the gate. We'd end our visit throwing rocks into mud puddles and at the seagulls that feasted on the raw garbage.

Uncle Eddie would stop us at the gate, inspect our finds, and pretend to calculate a price. He'd muster up a stern look and remind us that nothing was free in this world. We'd hold our breath, knowing that we didn't  have a penny between us, and wait for his price. He'd pause, straight-faced and then with a wink, wave us out, laughing.

That was my Uncle Eddie, always a smile, a joke, and a poke in the chest to say hello. I'd see him and Aunt Loretta and my three cousins for Christmas, Easter, and birthdays. I loved Uncle Eddie's stories and Aunt Loretta always gave me a big smack of a kiss on the cheek. Cousin Greg jazzed up the engines of his go-carts and motorbikes and raced them around his neighborhood. Once he built a model racetrack in his family's basement. He carted in dirt for the terrain, and hand-raced model cars, reenacting demolition derbies. The table was littered with wrecks and plastic car parts, which he'd rebuild and start all over again. Cousin Loretta, always the Beatles fan, would lead our family in dancing to the group's recent LP. Her younger brother, Eddie, the youngest and most agile of the three, would do flips out of whatever tree he was dangling from, and challenge us all to footraces that we all knew we'd lose to him. It was absolute joyous chaos when our families got together.

Sock Fights

When my cousin Mike slept over, which was either on a Friday or a Saturday every couple of months, we secretly looked forward to being sent off to bed. When we were tucked in and the lights were turned out, the sock wars would begin!

We'd wait to hear our moms' footsteps going down the stairs after wishing us a good night's sleep. The sound of chairs being dragged close to the kitchen table and the clinking of our parents' last cups of tea or coffee were background to the din of multiple conversations. This was their last occasion to talk national or family politics for the evening, and agree on pick-up times for my cousin after Sunday Mass and lunch. When we heard the *Goodbyes* exchanged at the front door, the slam of Aunt Dot's and Uncle Warren's car doors, we knew that battle trumpets would soon be sounding.

We'd take off our sleep socks and stuff them with the day's dirty underwear. I'd fish out clean socks and undies from my dresser and we'd push them deep into the feet of our socks. These were excellent bludgeons that we would swirl wildly overhead and bash one another without doing any serious harm.

If we were ambitious enough, we'd stretch an old pair beyond recognition and use, cramming a T-shirt as far into the sock as possible. This one would be a super mace with a Fruit of the Loom's underwear tag sticking out of the top of the hideously swollen garment.

We'd be knights, like those in the jousting scene from the movie, *El Cid*, bashing one another with spiked battle maces. We'd jump over pillows or use them as shields, rolling off the bed in a reenactment of dramatic death scenes. The sting of the full blows to the face lasted only seconds, and never interrupted our uncontrolled thrashing at one another. All was done as quietly as possible, sometimes in the dark, other times under the beams of the flashlights that I had hidden under my bed.

Sure, we'd always get out of hand, laughing or hitting the floor too hard, knocking a bedside lamp over or smashing against a wall. And then it would come, the high volume voice of authority, "Robert!!! Cut that out!"

I was no longer Bobby. I was Robert, and that was serious. Notice, it wasn't Michael's name shouted from the bottom of the stairs. He was the guest. So, when the battle was unleashed in his basement where we'd do sleepovers, a similar siren-like voice used his name. That was sleepover etiquette. We'd cover our laughs, get a few extra raps in, empty out our socks, and click off the flashlights.

Certainly, we'd spend our days like all the other kids, running the fields, battling dinosaurs or fighting off giant octopi from my picnic table. During inclement afternoon visits, we'd head down to the basement, build castles from wood blocks, and blast those miniature forts to pieces with a high-powered toy cannon that shot weighted, rubber-tipped, missile-shaped cannonballs.

That might sound deceptively simple, however it was anything but that. We'd pride ourselves on building the most blast-resistant structures possible out of store-bought or homemade blocks. Having the last castle standing did not assure one of victory. It wasn't about taking down the fort, it was all about survival, the survival of the number of plastic soldiers on our teams that remained standing. Our designs included safe rooms, enforced corners, and double-walled towers that might provide safe havens impervious to the impact of the cannon's shots. We kept score and bragged about our exploits through dinner. At least until our parents had heard enough, and we were told to finish whatever we had on our plates ... quietly. I typically left only smudges of my dinner, which must have been the explanation for my wearing kid-sized husky pants with the expandable waist.

However, my cousin Mike picked at his peas, ate them one by one,

83

and buried his meat in his mashed potatoes, nursing his glass of milk. I was advised to stay away from the table as he suffered through this. Peeking around the corner, I'd remind him of what was waiting for us; the much anticipated rubber-band gun battles.

We kids had been warned by parents and teachers never to shoot rubber bands at one another. *You'll lose an eye*, they'd say. Of course, we never listened, pulling them tight between thumb and forefinger and letting them fly. Shooting at one another or at innocent bystanders on the sly was common practice in school. At home, we'd just throw rocks.

But, my Uncle Warren one Christmas completely legitimized rubber band shooting, much to the chagrin of our moms, by presenting Mike and me with wooden pistols that fired rubber bands. Hand painted a light blue and lathe carved in his basement workshop, these pistols, accompanied by a package of rubber band *ammo*, provided entertainment for a good part of our childhood. His advisories made clear by a stern voice and a soul-piercing stare, Uncle Warren showed us how to load and discharge our gifts. Our plastic soldiers and toy animals bore the brunt of our improving marksmanship. We'd spend hours entertained by these magical simplicities.

During the heat of battle more than one errant shot would strike us, but by and large, we respected his rules and never deliberately shot one another or anyone else. We proudly showed off these cherished gifts to our friends, reciting the rules of use and conduct that Uncle Warren clarified for us that one Christmas.

His *Follow the rules and you'll have fun* echoed as we started to play. Sometimes rules were that easy to understand and get right.

Cigar Smoke Around the Table

Grandma Cross died in 1962, a year before Kennedy's assassination. I missed her very much. I stopped going to the Cross house in Huntington, and never watched wrestling again. I wasn't allowed to attend her wake and burial. So, I stayed home with my sister, Fran. Turns out that what happened at the wake rivaled what Grandma Cross and I used to watch on Saturdays.

My grandparents, John and Louise, had eleven children. Aunts Ronnie, Jeanie, Jessie, Dot, Alice and Uncles Eddie and Billy formed my living relations who I identified as the Cross family. Mom's brothers, John Francis Jr., Paul and Francis Thomas, I never knew. Paul passed before his first birthday, John Jr. died after his fourth year, and Francis Thomas died in a fire at the family home in Brooklyn at the age of two.

The remaining siblings, raised in Brooklyn, lived raucous, crisscrossing lives as children and young adults. Cross siblings shared beds; the three youngest girls in one and the two remaining boys in another. The nightly antics and teasing wouldn't stop until their dad appeared in the threshold with a belt in hand. Jean and Mary, the two oldest daughters, had aged out of sharing beds, but not a room. Jean found work and left home first. Mary, my mom, her younger siblings' caregiver, got the kids fed and off to school. John oversaw workers on Brooklyn dairy farms and had sundry other jobs, and Elizabeth laundered clothes for the neighbors.

Grandpa John Cross, born in 1887, and Grandma Louise Haupert

Cross, born a year later, Brooklynites, lived in Huntington the last twenty-five years of their lives. They came to many Sunday dinners at our house in East Northport. Grandma Louise Haupert Cross, raised on a family-run dairy farm in Brooklyn with her eight siblings, William, Jessie, Robert, Mary, Frederick, Daniel, Godfrey and John, had Scottish and German ancestry. My Mom spoke of the trolley ride her family would take to visit the Haupert clan "out in the sticks", Greenpoint, Brooklyn. The Cross children, urbanites all, ran wild through the farm's fields and barnyard. These family trips out to the countryside seemed to be one of Mom's most cherished childhood memories.

Between her accounts of playing with the cows and chickens and jumping out of the hayloft, Mom spoke of a family tragedy that happened on that farm. Irish childhood stories always seemed to have a dark lining to them.

It turned out that one afternoon when Louise was a child, she and her little brother, *Robby*, were playing hide-and-seek in the barn. Robert had hidden in a mound of hay. One of their uncles, pitching hay into the cow stalls, stabbed into the same mound with his pitchfork and struck little Robert. They discovered him when he started to bleed out. He died in the family living room.

My mom, Mary Louise, born in 1913, was one of the oldest of this clan, and during the Depression, at age sixteen, was the principal caregiver for her younger siblings, Dot, Billy, and Eddie. It was these three who I knew best. All of the Cross siblings, at least those that survived their childhoods, were Depression kids that shared beds and clothes, and had shoes whose withering soles they repaired with old newspapers.

Mom would go off to school every morning exhausted after making sure her siblings were dressed and fed. Once, she rested her head on a closed railroad crossing bar, and fell asleep. When the train passed, the bar rose, lifting her several feet in the air before she woke. She fell to the ground and landed on her face. With scratched cheeks and a swollen jaw, she was afraid to tell her parents that she had fallen asleep, and considered telling them that she had fought during recess. They might have excused the fight, but allowing yourself to be vulnerable by falling asleep in public, they surely wouldn't have forgiven. She told the truth and got whacked.

My grandpa John Cross worked as a foreman on a local dairy farm in Brooklyn. He carried a loaded gun to work everyday. John kept his great grandfather's shillelagh, the Irish walking stick, within reach, joking that it'd be useful just in case his kids got out of line. He was quite the storyteller when he'd take breaks from chain-smoking his stogies. Louise was the laundress for the neighbors.

According to Mom's stories, Uncles Eddie and Billy were neighborhood hellions, and rarely went to school. As young adults, Eddie joined the Air Force and Billy, the Submarine Service during World War II. They both survived, but not without their own personal reminders. Eddie had a gimp, which he said was due to the time he fell out of a plane during takeoff, and Billy, like so many other submarine men, suffered from serious trauma issues and acute insomnia. He passed away in California in his forties. Aunt Dot, the youngest of the living siblings, was always a respectful child and married Warren Delph, whose family was from the British-controlled Islands in the Caribbean. He did aerial reconnaissance for the OSS in the Pacific during the war.

Always in one another's hair in a drafty, three-bedroom, two-story house, childhood alliances and difficulties followed the Cross siblings into their adult lives. Apparently sometime during the last evening of Grandma Louise's wake at Jacobson's Funeral Parlor in Huntington, Mom and my Aunt Jean got into a fistfight. They had had a run-in two days before at the Huntington house, arguing over the distribution of mementos and photos, and family heirlooms. I never heard who separated them, but I always assumed it was Uncle Eddie. The account of Mom decking one of her sisters formed part of the Cross family history. These two adults, who in their early adulthood squared off frequently in a shared bedroom, would never see one another again.

We saw Grandpa John with more regularity after Grandma's death. He traveled with us to visit Fran at Notre Dame Catholic Women's College, which was outside of Baltimore, and on our frequent visits to D.C. He'd sit in the back of Dad's new Pontiac and smoke his cigars. Mom would always remind him to lower his backseat window. I'd lower mine and stick my head out as we traveled breakneck speed along those highways. Of course, Dad had license to smoke his stogies and Mom, her cigarettes. Ours was a smoking family, whose habit I never embraced. With our car filled with clouds of smoke during those long road trips, it was a miracle that I managed to survive!

Grandpa John passed in 1967. He was waked in Jacobson's, now a Cross family tradition. The last session before his burial, I sat in the back of the room with my cousin Mike. It was a much more tranquil event than Grandma's. All the Cross relatives except Aunt Jean who Mom had punched out, attended the party back at our home after his burial. I was sent over to a neighbor's house for ice cubes. I can remember that the music in our living room was loud, and we danced and laughed. That was how the Irish said their goodbyes.

The following night we all gathered at Aunt Dot and Uncle Warren's house for evening tea. John and Louise had spent their Sundays between our home and my cousin's for many years. Grandpa John had sat at their table hundreds of times, smoking away as always. That night we sat around my Aunt Dot's kitchen table in their finished basement, telling stories about John and Louise. Mike and I listened and laughed at the stories we'd heard many times before. It was the family's time to relive and laugh about my grandparent's antics. It struck me that no one was smoking. An evening tea spent with the Cross sisters was always accompanied by smoking cigarettes, but not that night.

Suddenly, Aunt Dot stopped talking and looked up. Everyone at the table went silent. We instinctively looked over to the doorway between the kitchen and the playroom. There was no one there, but the heavy smell of a lighted cigar advanced into the kitchen, approached our table, and slowly and very noticeably circled behind each of us.

"It's Daddy!" Aunt Dot, seated nearest the doorway, whispered.

Sure enough, each of us smelled his cigar smoke approach from behind and slowly dissipate as we sensed him walking around behind us. Uncle Warren was the last to smell the telltale scent of Grandpa Cross' stogie. As the odor traced off, each of us said our goodbyes to him. Mom and Aunt Dot were crying. I said, "Goodbye, Grandpa, and thanks for that day!"

No one knew what I was talking about.

One summer afternoon several years before, Grandpa John was driving the Cross cousins and me to Uncle Eddie's house in East Northport, off of Elwood Road. Eddie Jr., Loretta and I were crammed in the backseat and Greg sat next to him. Grandpa was in his glory, smoking and driving, his two most favorite activities outside of sitting in his easy chair watching ballgames. He seemed not to be bothered by our shouting, singing, and general roughhousing in the backseat.

At first we didn't notice how the car in the opposite lane started to drift over the yellow line into ours, heading straight for us. For kids as noisy as we were, we didn't say a word, just held our collective breath as we realized what was about to happen. It all transpired in seconds, but seemed like a slow-motion scene that we had seen on TV.

I watched the car approach us, thinking that we were all going to be killed. In the foreground was Grandpa John's sweaty, bald head, encircled by the familiar haze of cigar smoke. And in the blink of our eyes, certainly not his, he swerved to the right onto the grassy shoulder and avoided a head-on collision. As calmly as possible, not a word said, he turned back onto the road surface and continued along, taking puffs on his cigar, held tightly between his lips.

We kids erupted in cheers and applause, kissing him on his head and patting his shoulders. We cheered him and celebrated his driving prowess all the way to the Cross home. We pushed through the screen door, cheering, "Grandpa John saved us all! Grandpa John is our hero!" He said nothing about the incident, sat at the kitchen table, asked for a cold beer, and inquired about the score of the Yankee's game. *Just another day in the life of a grandpa*, he must have thought.

So, I thanked him for the day he saved us, that night when he came back to say goodbye, and share a smoke with his family one more time.

This Too Will Pass

It was all about the closet.

Whether ajar or completely closed, there was something in there, *someone* in there. Wooden sliding doors covered this dark pit. Conceived as a utilitarian space, it now became an absolutely terrifying, timeless vortex. Housing my clothes and the larger toys that didn't fit in my toy chest, the shadowy sliver of black lurking behind its parted doors haunted my nightly battles with exhaustion and my need to be vigilant. Ever alert to the slightest movements or whispers behind them, my eyes never left the closet doors. I would fall asleep with sheets clasped tightly, drawn up below my nose. I was six years old when I met what hid behind those closet doors.

My first visit to our new house off of Pulaski Road in this Suffolk County community was during a Saturday drive. Mom and Dad coaxed me into the car with the promise of ice cream and some trinket if I behaved during the long car ride. I watched our Glen Cove house disappear as I hunkered down in the backseat of Dad's Dodge. I fell into sleep's time machine and we arrived in minutes.

Adjacent to an expanse of furrowed fields, the wood framed homes, like pages in a child's coloring book, were in various stages of completion. As we slowed down, I noticed a shuttered, ramshackle farmhouse partially hidden behind the overgrowth of vines and wild cherry trees in the woods across from the corner of the new development. An old woman watched us from the shadows of her collapsing front porch of her two-story farmhouse as we turned down what I'd come to call *my street.*

Dad headed down the unpaved, dirt roadway demarcated by newly poured cement curbs. Dump trucks and cement mixers made their way past work crews who dangled from scaffolding and hammered in the recesses of my future neighbors' homes. We pulled into the rain-puddled and rutted entrance that would become our asphalted driveway.

As the final touches to our three-story house were being made, my folks had decided to do this walk-through, surely hoping that their $13,000 investment in our family's happiness was justified. Ours was to be the first completed and first occupied house on the block. The construction site appeared closed to the public, but we walked through the doorless garage into what would be a playroom and up to the first floor. My folks got distracted in the kitchen. I wandered around the shell, smelling the freshly cut wood. I heard movement and muffled voices of workers upstairs.

Several of the workmen who were heading off to their lunch break advised me to be careful. The last worker, coveralls stained with some kind of shiny grease, cautioned, gesturing up to the second floor, that some of the rooms had yet to be sheet-rocked and that nails and 2x4 wood scraps littered the floor. And whatever I did, he made very clear; that I was to stay out of the unfinished bathroom. Turned out, he said, that a stray dog had given birth to a litter of puppies in the bathtub and dragged her afterbirth over the edge of the tub when she exited.

I made a beeline up the stairs in the chance that there'd be a puppy left over ... had no idea what afterbirth was, didn't much care. Running past the carpenters' bibs, buckets of nails, and cigarette butts, I poked my head into a small room. Pipes stuck out of the wall and there was a hole to connect a toilet. A bathtub, partially covered with cardboard, dust, and random globs of spackle, had a smear of dried and flaking crimson that stained its side from the tub's lip to the floor. Wads of crumpled up newspaper piled in the corner had been used to scoop something up.

I tiptoed in ... no puppies.

Stepping out into the hall, my steps sounded hard on the exposed plywood floor, echoing up through the rafters. So, this was to be our family's new home.

My brother and sister would share a landing that led to ample bedrooms on the third floor. A few years later when my brother went off to the Navy, we kept that room clean and unused, waiting for his return. My sister had a wall full of easterly facing windows and a walk-in closet, lighted by a pull chain from a single light socket.

Being the *baby* of the family, I was given the smallest bedroom down the hall from my parent's and adjacent to the bathroom. Its two windows overlooked the farm fields that led the rising moon's light directly to my pillow. A large framed-out closet space where sliding doors would close and hide things away filled the corner. At first glance, that rectangular alcove seemed harmless. Not yet outfitted with its sliding doors, it was simply an uninspiring nook, its wicked nature still undiscerned.

After moving in, we accommodated ourselves to this newly constructed home in this model neighborhood, off the potato fields of East Northport. Our first days in the house, I'd sit in my closet and close the door, pretending that I was in a submarine.

And then I heard the noises.

They seemed to come from the trap door that led to the attic through the ceiling of my closet. Light framed its outline. I didn't understand why there was any light there. Maybe it was the sunlight poking though the vents in the sides of the house. Sitting in that darkened space, I heard movement. The light that filtered down through the cracks of the trap door shimmered. There couldn't possibly be anyone up there. I stepped out and quietly closed the sliding door.

I never sat in there again, at least not alone.

My room had to be kept clean of toys, definitely no clothes on the floor, everything put away and hung on hangers. This was part of the responsibility of having my own room, I was told. Simple, straight-lined furniture pieces filled the space; a dresser sandwiched between the door to the room and the closet's left sliding door, a desk near the corner windows, a twin bed positioned directly across from the closet and a toy chest against the wall that adjoined my parent's room. With my pillows bunched up, I'd lean on my elbows and see the moon rise directly over the distant tree line. Its cold, reflected light poured across the potato field.

But it was the closet that soon became my focus.

At first, I heard a shifting sound somewhere from behind my clothes, very subtle, almost like a whisper of leaves rustling down a street. Behind the hushed swishing of clothes being moved aside, I could hear a movement of metal hangers being slowly pulled along the closet's wooden clothes bar. And then it'd stop, teasing me to believe that it wasn't real. Couldn't be in this new neighborhood, this new house! Certainly this closet was just that, a new closet. With eyes and ears focused on those closet doors, I waited. Nothing.

Every night I heard the barely perceptible shuffling of clothes and rasping of hangers. At least until the Thursday of the second week in our home, when through the shadows the closet door closest to me appeared to slightly shift open. I didn't move, keeping my body as rigid as a board. Like flicking my finger over an open flame, I focused on the dark pitch between the door and the closet's molding, trying to penetrate the blackness and hoping not to see anything, but almost wishing I would. There had to be something, someone there.

That night I knew I had to move, but couldn't bring myself to make the slightest movement. It might rush me if I did. Yet if I didn't move, the door might continue to open. I couldn't have that. I jumped from the bed to the light switch and instantly there was light. The closet door was closed. The house was dark, my family asleep. I sat on the floor near the hallway door, leaned against the wall, and fell asleep.

The next day after dinner, I insisted that the bed be moved so that the head of my bed would be against the wall I shared with my parent's room. So, with my door open, I could see into the hallway illuminated by the bathroom's nightlight, all the way up to the third floor. It was a short run out my door and a quick turn to the left into my parents' room.

The toy chest, hinged and sharply rectangular, contained only the select few of my toys that helped make falling asleep easier. Placed to the left of the head of my bed, parallel to the wall, it's location provided easy access for clandestine playtime at night. Sometimes it proved invaluable in distracting me from those closet doors. There was the occasional night when I'd fall asleep holding my stuffed monkey or some handful of plastic cowboys and Indians pulled from that chest. Those nights the closet was simply part of the wall.

During the third month, my parents awoke to my screams. They said that I must have turned in my sleep and fallen out of bed, splitting open my eyelid and forehead on one of the toy chest's corners. I remember waking up on the floor, feeling the sting of a hot poker on my right eye, and tasting warm liquid in my mouth. Mom and Dad bundled me up and rushed me off to Huntington Hospital. They cursed that toy chest and its sharp corners and would later move it under my corner window. I remember the trip in my car's dark backseat, clutching my blanket and wondering how I could tell them that it wasn't my fault, that I didn't roll out of bed. *She* had cut me.

That night I remember falling asleep and dreaming that a wooden lady had pulled the door open and sat across from my bed, tapping her nails on the floor, watching me sleep. She'd stand in a blink and drift over to the foot of my bed where she'd weave back and forth, stretching out her fingers and those long, pointed nails.

I could see her well now. Dressed in a shadow, a form hidden in black, her face was that of a wooden mannequin, black eyes and nose, a mouth painted lipstick-red, articulated arms like a hideous marionette and her hands with sharpened knuckles, pulsing wooden fingers that flexed with enormous, splinter-like fingernails.

And then I was on the floor and there was blood.

They couldn't use anesthesia for some reason that night in the hospital. As the surgeon leaned over me and pushed the needle through the skin above the tear in the flesh under my eyebrow, I started to scream, kick and tried to sit up. The attending nurses didn't seem to expect me to be so strong, so intent on going home, even if it meant going back to the room with the closet.

"Doctor, help us please!" a voice came from what I thought was the corner of the operating table. I saw bright, green lights, white coats and gloved hands that cupped my face as I shook back and forth and screamed for my parents.

I remember the nurse insisted that the second doctor help hold me down as the surgeon continued to stitch me up like some kind of child puppet. The needle started to push through easier and quicker. I didn't stop kicking until the white masked face, whose eyes squinted, angry with my resistance, had pulled back. I heard the snap of rubber gloves. He announced that he was done as he moved past me and moved out the door.

I spent the night in a room with another boy whose head I saw poking above the sheets as they rolled me in past his bed. The lighted hall's shadows flickered with the passing of the nurse on duty, an electric, tinkle-bell sound broke the quiet, a doctor was paged, a child was crying down the hall. There were no closets in this room. I fell asleep.

My parents knew of my fears, knew that I felt something else lived in their new home, my new home. They never dismissed my concerns, and, of course, commiserated with me, but explaining away this inexplicable reality stymied them. I suspected that they suffered at the hands of unrelenting jobs and schedules and their requisite weekday absence. I'm sure they felt overwhelmed by all of that. The best they could do was reassure me and hope that I grew out of it.

When I turned seven, they asked me if I thought I still needed my babysitter. I didn't say no. It was the closet, you know. When we moved in, they asked our only neighbor at the time, Macey, to watch over me for the duration of the school year. Her son had become my first friend on the block. So, through the first grade, she sent me off in the morning with her *Be good today, Bobby* and was there when I put the key in the door in the afternoon. Macey was with me all that school year and through the summer, keeping my closet's occupant at bay.

It was the end of that summer and I was going into the second grade when my parents sat me down in the kitchen one August evening. I knew the question was coming. Did I want Macey to watch over me for another school year. I told them no, that I'd be fine, knowing that in the darkest corner of that closet … *she* chuckled mutedly.

I would be alone to face her.

The house was a chameleon that changed its semblance as soon as my parents went off to work. I stayed home alone, making my breakfast, getting ready for the day, and locking up as I headed out to Fifth Avenue Elementary School. The house seemed to know just when to let its wood whimper, an upstairs tread creak, a shade rustle or a door slowly close. It was a house that wore a mask. For the holidays, on weekends or parents' days off, when family and friends came over, its hands, warm and supportive, held us all. But this house's presence intuited when they were gone; parents back to work, visiting relatives and friends returned to their homes and me ... alone.

Then the house's countenance changed, it became something else, someone else. I spent a lot of time alone in the house. Rainy overcast days were the worst. With plenty of sunny, summer days and friends waiting in the back lot to decide what adventure we'd have that day, I never went home until my parents returned. I'd head back just before 5:30 in the afternoon. Sometimes, I'd sit on the stoop, waiting outside. School vacations were dreadful, particularly in the winter. And as much as I hated school, I couldn't wait to get back and away from *her*.

I never talked to any of my buddies about the house or the presence. They all had houses that looked like mine. Why would mine be different? So, I'd have to get tough, endure the winter when I wasn't out sleigh riding, wrestling in the snow or snowball fighting. I'd put the T.V. on low and listen for things coming down from upstairs.

Sometimes I'd be in the kitchen when I heard noises on the second or third floors. I'd grab a carving knife that I'd usually only see during Thanksgiving. Dad, dressed in a white shirt and tie for that holiday, would proudly carve the white meat in symmetrical sheaves. He'd sharpen that knife till it glistened. How I loved Thanksgiving, but hated seeing that knife. It reminded me of what was waiting for me the following week when all returned to their routines. The noises would return and I'd have to scramble for that knife in a moments notice. I thought that I could somehow threaten it out of the house, by shouting it out, walking around the house brandishing that knife. I'd stomp up the stairs, announce my coming, and tell it to get out of *my* house.

No one ever answered, she knew better.

After all, this was really *her* house.

My parents could see it on my face when they'd come home. When was I going to learn that the banging was just the hot water pipes or that new houses settled and creaked … that no one was in the attic? But they didn't know what it was like to sit in the playroom, waiting to hear something moving on the second floor, then on the first, just out of sight, coming down the stairs, around the nearest corner, feet away from me. I decided I could survive this and vowed never to tell them about the noises, the whispers, the feelings ever again. I certainly wouldn't tell them about *her*.

She was in the closet. I knew she was there, always at night. In the morning I'd slide open the closet door to get dressed and she'd be gone. The morning light burned into the corner of that closet, cleaning it of her essence. But she lingered, up in the attic, her lair. At night, every night, I'd hear her shifting behind the closed doors that I had pulled fully closed before getting into bed. I'd lay there in the dark, staring at the door closest to me, and watch it be slowly drawn open. Just enough for her to look out, just enough for her to slip her long, sharpened wooden nails around the door's edges, clicking them on the molding's varnished surface. I'd sit up in a panic and turn on the light. The door would be closed just like I had left it only minutes before. But in the dark I knew I could see the door shifting open and then her talons would inch around the doorframe, slowly pulling the closet's door open. I'd be asleep only after repeatedly checking the door and then laying in wait for any movement.

Aunt Mae came to visit around the holidays. Down from Hartford, Connecticut where she lived in a rented room and worked for Muscular Dystrophy, her visits offered me an oasis of hugs, Slap Jack card games and soothing conversations. Aunt Mae's translucent white skin and boney frame were always covered by well-ironed dresses. Her white lace handkerchiefs stuck out from her sweater's pocket. She half whispered her conversations, gently caressing my hair. Her sweater had the scent of perfume and mothballs. Her drawn, smiling face and her weary eyes reflected her kindness. Peace had come with Aunt Mae. No noises now.

But there still was the closet. It was with my Aunt Mae that I shared these stories, these fears knowing that she would stroke the top of my hand. She never once said that it was impossible, that these were just dreams, just simply a child's imaginings. Aunt Mae counseled me saying, "Just like so many other things in life, Bobby, this too will pass."

And so, I invited her to sit with me in the closet.

We didn't tell my parents. Up to my room, sliding open one of the doors, we made room by moving toys and shoes and sat down in the shadows. I told her everything. She listened without interruption, with the face of a believer who glanced up at the trap door while I spoke. It was logical, I told her, that if the wooden lady couldn't be found in the closet, she had to be up in the attic. That would be her world.

I heard my mother's voice calling us.

"Shhh … let's stay here," she whispered.

"Don't worry, you're with your Auntie Mae."

They finally found us huddled together, laughing.

Aunt Mae was the oldest surviving sibling of my father, nevertheless she was gently reprimanded that day for encouraging me, for reinforcing every fear I had, for humoring me. *And how could you sit in that closet with him,* she'd be asked.

We were quiet at dinner.

Aunt Mae never asserted herself, and would only politely direct conversation when appropriate. But that night she looked at her younger brother and told him to get a ladder and look up there and see where that light was coming from. So, he did.

Access to the trap door required shifting the clothes, wedging between the top shelf and the doorframe, and pushing open the two-foot square trap door to see into the cavernous attic. It ran the length of the house. Cotton candy-like insulation was visible above the floor joists and a row of plywood flooring ran from the trap door opening to the end of the attic, stopping below the attic vent in the peak of the inside wall. The corners and sides of the house pinched down by the roof rafters disappeared into the shadows. No outside light from this sunny Saturday penetrated there.

With a *Here, look. See, nothing at all,* my dad flashed the beam of the flashlight around the attic, its light barely reaching the attic's outer corners. I climbed up the ladder and looked in, holding the flashlight, straining to see if I could see her shape hunched down in the dark.

I waited to hear the clicking of her nails ... silence.

Too many shadows, too many indiscernible forms, I was unconvinced, but didn't let on. I couldn't let Aunt Mae lose face. I explained that she came out only at night. I was about to insist that we repeat this exploration at night, but I was afraid the moment that Dad pulled back the trap door, she'd be perched on its edge, nails ready to slice us.

My father assured, "There's nothing's there and you saw for yourself. Right?"

Unconvinced, I nodded agreement. *Right, Dad, nothing there.*

My aunt's visit ended. We returned to the routine of work and school, but the nights continued dark and foreboding as always. And they thought that looking up in the attic would reveal her darkened corner lair! She wouldn't allow that.

And so the wooden lady visited whenever she wanted, clicking her nails and drifting slowly up to stand by my bed. In spite of her, life moved on as my aunt had assured.

Over the course of the following years she came less frequently. Christmases, Easters, birthday celebrations, family gatherings and parties, and advancing through elementary and junior high schools quieted her presence. Making phone calls to girlfriends replaced throwing dirt bombs. The years had passed. Her presence had waned.

And then it was time for us to sell the house.

The morning we moved out, I peeked into my old bedroom. The closet doors were shut. When I entered junior high and my brother had married, I moved up to his room on the third floor, quieter and more private, better for studying and daydreaming. The closet there was just a closet.

The last day our house echoed, empty of furniture. All the boxes had been collected and sent en route across town. I stood there in the silence, my parents waiting in the car. I told them that I had forgotten something.

The house stood quiet.

Memories flooded back. Every party, family gathering, my cousins and I dancing in the living room to the Beatles, discovering Christmas trees at dawn, the sing-alongs my sister's friends would have, my brother standing at the door in his sailor's uniform, all of us in tears as his leave ended, my sister in her robe carrying our dog Tex down the stairs with curlers in his fur, the conversations, jokes, and arguments at the dinner table, the many windows I'd accidentally broken, carving pumpkins and returning here after roaming the streets on Halloweens, every word said, and those never given voice in these halls and rooms. Everything was here, even the closet.

I remembered my Aunt Mae whispering, "This too will pass, Bobby."

The car's horn broke the silence. I moved down the stairs to the playroom. At the door to the garage, I stopped and waited, listening.

A stair rung creaked, and a clicking from upstairs, a clicking on the floor where my childhood bedroom once was, echoed through the playroom. Like the tapping of a stowaway, trapped in the hold of a sinking ship that drifted into the ocean's blackness, something seemed to signal.

The pipes … for sure.

Stepping out into the garage, I smiled, closed and locked that door for the last time, and left that house bare of memories. Crumpled, smeared or folded neatly, I took them all, even her, to share with you.

A Word or Two

What will it be like
To realize that the last time that I'll say your name
Has arrived.

Will I be able to force my voice to be strong,
Summon words that you can hold in your memory's hand,
Look into your eyes with a smile as I leave,
Be firm in my need to give you strength as I lose mine.
And remember not to say goodbye
Nor hint at your mortality by saying that we'd
see one another again some day.

Of any words to be shared
In my heart I know I'd want to say *Thank you*
For your love, your presence, for allowing our lives and those of
yours to rub together in the myriad of ways that they have,
And for your patience with my fumbling through this life,

If I could, I'd ask you to remember to remember ... me.
To share recollections
And to laugh at, with, and because of me,
And keep close a word or two of mine.
And remember to say my name
From time to time.

Sound Beach
August, 2019

Other works by the author

Hodum's collection of horror tales, **Bone Dust,** depicts a world where ravenously deranged homesteads breathe, shape shift, and consume the unwitting, vengeful contagions turn on their makers, afflictions from ancient rituals endure, death refuses to step from your door, and a child's nursery rhyme unfolds time. Embark on a shadowy journey through alternate realities where the macabre, haunting childhood fears, and ghostly entities await. Twisted encounters in these unsettling and frightening personal worlds will seem so alarmingly possible and disturbingly real. Step through this portal and find yourself reflected in the whispering silhouettes that follow you through the pages of these tales. Available through BookBaby and Amazon.

Catching Winds North, a collection of the author's poetry, celebrates the seasons and beauty of Long Island, nature's mysteries, and the joys and conundrums of life. This work includes poetry inspired by the author's life in Colombia, his travels to Ecuador and Peru, and his mission work in Nicaragua. His writings about his life abroad appear in the original Spanish with English translations. Available through iUniverse and Amazon.

In *Conversations on La Playa: A Gringo's Tales of Medellin,* journey to a country so blessed with breathtaking landscapes, yet torn by poverty and civil unrest, and travel through some of Colombia's most unforgettable and magical settings. As an American exchange student in the early 1970s, Hodum lived in Medellín, Colombia and traveled through Cordillera mountain ranges, mysterious jungles and deserts, enduring the travails of life on the road through one of South America's most exciting countries. With candor, heartfelt insight and humor, Hodum recreates all the joys, tragedies, unique personalities, and sights and sounds of the Colombia he came to know and love. He recounts his life-changing experiences and many adventures in mist-enshrouded Cordillera neighborhoods, and the haunting and unforgettable street people of the urban landscape of Medellín, the City of the Eternal Spring. Available through iUniverse and Amazon.

Pilgrims' Steps: A Search for Spain's Santiago is an examination of the life of St. James the Greater and the origins and history of the *Camino de Santiago*, the Spanish pilgrimage route dedicated to this apostle. The author's many trips to Spain inspired him to walk the pilgrimage route and investigate the saint's life. After having traveled the route to Santiago de Compostela, he resolved to provide today's pilgrims with a clearer understanding of who the namesake of the Spanish pilgrimage route might have been. Available through iUniverse and Amazon.

Printed in the United States
by Baker & Taylor Publisher Services